Encounteri

CHRIS HUGHES

ERIES EDITOR: SIMON J ROBINSON

DayOne

© Day One Publications 2011
First printed 2011

978–1–84625–298–3

British Library Cataloguing in Publication Data available

Published by Day One Publications
Ryelands Road, Leominster, HR6 8NZ
Telephone 01568 613 740   FAX 01568 611 473

email—sales@dayone.co.uk
web site—www.dayone.co.uk

Cover design by Kathryn Chedgzoy
Printed by Thomson Litho, East Kilbride

The neglected Bible includes books like Ezra. Tucked away in the Old Testament is a record of how a largely unseen God moves through world events, demonstrating that he is mighty to save. Chris Hughes has worked to understand and apply the message of a book that does not need to remain neglected.

Declan Flanagan, Chief Executive, Rural Ministries, UK

Can God be trusted? That's one of the ultimate questions for people exploring the Christian faith. In short pithy chapters, Chris Hughes shows us that God is working it all out according to plan—his story and ours. And he does it through ordinary people like Ezra who find themselves caught up in God's extraordinary purposes. This short book will deepen your confidence in God and whet your appetite to get involved in the biggest drama in history.

Richard Underwood, Pastoral Director, The Fellowship of Independent Evangelical Churches (FIEC), UK

Chris Hughes has made the book of Ezra come alive for the modern reader. It is full of useful historical background, with great illustrations and application for our lives today and many references to other biblical passages that make it a must for teachers and preachers. It is a challenge and an encouragement to all who are seeking to serve Christ in difficult times.

Jim Winter, Author and Pastor, UK

Contents

Introduction

Robin and Batman, Watson and Sherlock Holmes, Tonto and the Lone Ranger (or even Little John and Robin Hood)—is Ezra only to be seen as Nehemiah's 'sidekick': always in his shadow, the hors d'œuvre to Nehemiah's main course?

I was reminded of this perception when speaking to someone recently who commented that he was surprised Ezra warranted a book in his own right; he would expect, at best, a book about both Ezra and Nehemiah.

However, God's using of Ezra—especially in one particular incident—has thrilled me over many years. Whether that sense of amazement will be captured in this book I must leave you to decide; but I hope that you will at the very least come away with a certainty that as 'God's revival man' Ezra was much more than simply someone else's sidekick.

1 Gaining insight from God's notebook

(Ezra 1:1–4)

CASUALTY

For a number of years my mother suffered from an infrequent but agonizing condition. From time to time the muscles in her upper neck and lower face would go into spasm and her jaw would spontaneously dislocate. It was horribly painful when it happened, and there was no solution other than for her to be taken to the casualty department (A&E or ER) of the hospital and for her to have her jaw manipulated back into place.

As this happened both when she was at home and when she was staying with either my brother's family or mine, we became quite regular visitors to casualty departments across central-southern England—Southampton, Winchester, Frimley near Camberley and Guildford. If they had given frequent-flyer miles for trips to casualty, we would have clocked up quite a few between us in the years before a long-term solution was achieved.

We became very familiar with what was happening to my mother and what would need to be done to resolve the problem. Often the doctors were confronted with something they had never come across before and, consequently, they had no experience that would indicate to them what needed doing and how to do it. We also learnt that, no matter which hospital we were visiting, there was either within or very close to every casualty department a facility for taking X-rays—a means of allowing the medical staff to see beyond what they could see with their eyes, feel with their hands or hear with their ears.

EXAMINING HISTORY

The book of Ezra is a bit like an X-ray machine. The events recorded for us in Ezra fall into a period of history which is well documented in many ways and by many writers, some of whom were all but contemporaries. Indeed, as I write I have on my desk two books which speak of the kings and kingdoms mentioned in the book of Ezra, such as Cyrus, Persia, Babylon, Xerxes and Darius. The first is *The Histories*,[1] written by Herodotus, who is often described as the 'father of history' and who lived at almost the same time as Ezra. The other book, *Persian Fire*, has a 2005 copyright date.[2] Both books give us great insight into and understanding of the events of those days and the political and military forces that shaped human history.[3]

However, there is one thing that the book of Ezra does that those two books do not do—something that would be impossible for either of the authors of those two books to do without the insight given by God through Ezra (and the corresponding insight in 2 Chr. 36:22–23). For God, through the book of Ezra, takes us beneath the skin of human history to lay bare both the heart of Cyrus—telling us how he was moved by God to take the action that he did—and the underlying purposes of God which were being worked out through Cyrus and those who would follow him:

In the first year of Cyrus king of Persia, in order to fulfil the word of the Lord spoken by Jeremiah, the Lord moved the heart of Cyrus king of Persia to make a proclamation throughout his realm and to put it in writing ... (Ezra 1:1)

OTHER HISTORY

Here right at the beginning of this book is a clear reminder of two great certainties. Firstly, we see that God is at work in human history. Then, secondly, we see that we can never fully hope to understand all that is happening in history without the benefit of God's divine perspective and insight. Indeed, as many preachers have reminded their congregations through the years, history is 'His story'.

These two certainties are revealed to us again and again in the pages of God's Word, the Bible. We see it on the great stage of world and national events—from the cataclysmic days of the flood and the reasons that lay behind that worldwide calamity, to the consequences that flowed from the placing of a single Jewish boy in a papyrus basket in a location where he would be found by the daughter of the ruler of Egypt (see Gen. 6:1–8 and Exod. 2:1–10). We are shown God at work in and through the lives of individuals, and we see how he takes apparently insignificant life stories and weaves them into his glorious and eternal plans for the universe. (If you have never spent time looking at the lives mentioned in Matthew 1—and not just the 'headline' names of Abraham and David—it is an exercise that repays itself in many ways.)

A Greek philosopher once claimed, 'Give me a lever long enough and a fulcrum on which to place it, and I shall move the world.'[4] God, however, has throughout history moved both the world and the course of world history according to his eternal will—using as his instruments imperfect, fault-ridden and fallen human beings. And among those instruments in his hands were the empire-builders known as Cyrus and Darius.

LOOKING AT LIFE FROM BOTH SIDES NOW

As we look at history—which can be as recent as half a nanosecond ago—what do we use to help us understand, interpret and respond to the events which have been and are taking place in the world around us? Those events could be on the world stage—earthquakes, famines, wars and rumours of war. Or they may be situations that unfold in the personal lives of people very close and dear to us and which shake homes and families. It is said that the benefit of hindsight gives us perfect (60/60) vision. Yet you only have to read a few books about complicated or controversial events in human history to realize that what for one historian is 60/60 vision is for another the fog of war.[5]

It is only God who both knows the end from the beginning and also looks on the heart and not just the outward appearance (Isa. 46:10; 1 Sam. 16:7). It is only God who is, in the words of a wonderful old hymn, working his purpose out as year succeeds to year.

THEN

The book of Ezra starts in about 559 BC by drawing back the curtain of history to show God's hand at work behind the designs of a mighty emperor. It reveals God honouring the promises he made through the prophet Jeremiah to bring his people back from exile after seventy years (Jer. 29:10–11). Looking at those same promises brought the prophet Daniel to his knees, pleading with God to do as he had promised (Dan. 9:1–3).

Earlier, Moses also understood what had happened in his lifetime in terms of the promises of God being fulfilled. So at the end of his life he recalled what God had said: 'See, I have given you this land. Go in and take possession of the land that the LORD swore he would give to your fathers—to Abraham, Isaac and Jacob—and to their descendants after them' (Deut. 1:8).

These are just a few examples of people in Bible times who understood that their lives were being lived in the light of a God of promises.

NOW

But what about us today? We are not part of a people returning from slavery—on a forty-year journey home to the Promised Land. Nor do we live at the end of the seventy-year period promised by God through the prophet Jeremiah.

But we share with these Bible characters two keys to the world in which we live:

- God has not changed: he remains a God who makes and keeps his promises.
- Like these men and women in the Bible, we live in a time of exile/slavery; and just as there was for them an exodus/return from exile which God had promised, so there is for us, and that promise is being fulfilled.

PROBLEM

The problem is that we rarely have the capacity to contemplate the full force of such exile/exodus. For the time period of our 'exile' is the whole of human history, and the whole of the universe is affected (see Rom. 8:22—'whole creation').

This exile is an exile from God—an exile caused by the rejection of God (sin) by our first parents and perpetuated by our innate and ongoing rejection of him, so that Paul could say with utter clarity that 'There is no one righteous, not even one; there is no one who understands, no one who seeks God' (Rom. 3:10–11). Thus the 'return' is a return to God—a return that starts here on earth but which will find its full and perfect expression around God's throne in the new heaven and new earth that has yet to be revealed (see Rev. 21, for example).

And in this exile/exodus there are also crucial promises, the crux of which focuses on the events of three days in and around Jerusalem at about AD 30. These promises are to be found throughout the Bible, as Jesus reminded his followers on his resurrection day (Luke 24:25–27, 44–46).

It is the message of the crucified and risen Christ and our response to him (repentance, leading to his forgiveness) that we are to know for ourselves and proclaim to others (Luke 24:46–47).

We are no longer in the world in which Ezra lived, in the sense that we no longer have God revealing his hand at work with canonical authority. However, like Ezra, we do have God's revelation of the future unfolding of history which, like the promises made through Jeremiah, reveals how his plans and purposes are being and will be worked out until the time comes for the world in which we live to be made anew, with a new heaven and a new earth.

We do not have a specific time period akin to the seventy years from Jeremiah's day. But God has most certainly confirmed that the time period in which we live will come to an end—on a day and at an hour known by our Father in heaven—and that, until that day comes, we live in a time when men and women, young and old, have the opportunity to hear about and respond to the good news of God's Son, who is the Saviour. The key name, the name that matters above all others in this day, does not belong to a human king, president, prince or emperor; it is the name of the King of kings and Prince of Peace: the Lord Jesus Christ.

CROSS WORDS

Ezra reminds us that we are to see history in the light of God's promises. I need to ask myself, Do I try, as best I can, to look at today's events—whether world disasters or personal tragedies—in the light of God's promises, and supremely through the lens of the crucifixion and resurrection of Jesus Christ?

Over recent days I have found myself looking again at an old, but nevertheless helpful, way of seeing the symbol of a cross in three ways. A cross usually looks like this: X.

Firstly, I am old enough to remember the days when incorrect sums at school ($2 + 2 = 7$, for example) would be marked with an X to show that there was something wrong. And the cross reminds us of just how wrong things are in this fallen world, a world corrupted and affected in every part by sin.

So when we see or hear of some event that smacks of sin in any form, it should not take us by surprise. Instead, it should remind us of God's accurate assessment of the deepest need of all men and women around the world.

There is a risk, however, that this idea of sin appears too commonplace, impersonal or vague. The sin which took Jesus to the cross was not the nebulous or generic sin of humanity; it was the sin of me—and of you. One song says that 'It was my sin that held him there …'[6]

A cross, secondly, can appear at the end of a letter, card or valentine, symbolizing a kiss and demonstrating one person's love for another. We see this love at the crucifixion too.

Whether a cross is drawn like an X, a + or ✝, one thing is clear: the cross is just that: a cross. It is empty.

It is empty because Jesus completed his eternal work of salvation once for all on the cross, by giving his own life that we might have eternal life in him. And it is empty because he went from the cross to the grave, and three days later rose again as the One to whom all authority in heaven and on earth has now been given (Matt. 28:18).

We live in the world of the empty cross and the empty tomb: a world in which our Saviour is today seated on his throne in glory, beside his (and our, if we are Christians) Heavenly Father. Until he returns he will be there as our Advocate who speaks for us and prays for us to our Father in heaven.

Yet how often I get bogged down by the situations which get between my mind and heart and the wonder of my risen Saviour! How privileged I have been to spend time with God's people, whose hearts and minds have been anchored firm and sure in the knowledge of God—through spending time with him where he is today.

A third way of using a cross is on a Jolly Roger (the pirates' flag) or a map with an X clearly marked on it. For the cross reminds us of a treasure—a treasure of such wealth that it is worth selling all we have to acquire it (Matt. 13:44).

Yet the wonder of this treasure is that:

- We don't have to dig for it—it is a gift freely given from the hands of our life-giving Saviour.
- We don't have to search for it—it is 'near you; it is in your mouth and in your heart' (Rom. 10:8; Paul goes on to explain that this refers to believing in and confessing who Christ is and what he has done for us).
- It can never be taken away from us—not by a pirate or a king; for it comes from the King of kings himself, and nothing can separate us from the love of God in Christ Jesus (Rom. 8:39).

We will see in the following chapters that Ezra lived his life in the light of God's promises. May we all know the security and joy of living like this.

1. Can you think of other times in either the Old or the New Testament when God's people or the leaders of God's people might have had reason to doubt God's sovereign control?

2. Read the prayers of Ezra's contemporaries in Nehemiah 1 and Daniel 9. What gave them the confidence to pray and act as they did? In particular, how was Daniel influenced by the reading of God's Word?

3. In the Garden of Gethsemane, at the time of Jesus's arrest, who was in control? Whose plans were being worked out and whose promises were fulfilled (Matt. 26:54, 56)? When Peter preached to the crowd on the Day of Pentecost, whose purposes did he recognize behind the crucifixion of Christ (Acts 2:23)?

TO THINK ABOUT AND DISCUSS

1. If, following your study of the above passages, you were asked, 'Has God changed since then?' would you have any hesitation in giving an answer? What might or does cause such hesitation?
2. How might Daniel's approach assist us today?

Notes

1 **Herodotus,** *The Histories*, tr. Robin Waterfield (Oxford: Oxford World's Classics (n.d.)).
2 **Tom Holland,** *Persian Fire* (London: Abacus, 2005).
3 The Cyrus Cylinder, which can be found in the British Museum in London, is another example. It speaks of Cyrus 'restoring [people] to their dwellings', and it is thought that it was an early example of political propaganda following Cyrus's conquest of Babylon. See, for example, www.livius.org/a/1/inscriptions/cyrus.pdf.
4 **Archimedes,** cited at www.brainyquote.com.
5 See 'Fog of War' at en.wikipedia.org.
6 From **Stuart Townend,** 'How Deep the Father's Love for Us', 1995.

2 Ezra's reviving moment

(Neh. 8:1–9)

CHARLIE BROWN'S DREAM

In *Nobody's Perfect, Charlie Brown* the cartoonist Charles M. Schulz records a conversation between Charlie Brown and his friend Linus. Charlie Brown says, 'Here's something I think about quite often ... I'm sitting in the stands at the ball game, see ... Suddenly a line drive is hit my way ... Everybody ducks, but I stick up my hand, and make a great catch!

'The manager of the home team sees me and yells, "SIGN THAT KID UP!"'

'Have you ever heard of anyone else having that dream?'

To which Linus replies, 'Only about thirty billion other kids!'[1]

I'm not sure if there is an equivalent dream for those who are or long to be involved in God's work. Perhaps it might be of someone sitting in a large church or Christian meeting, only to hear that the preacher is unwell, and the cry goes up, 'Is there a preacher in the house?'

For some, their dream may be that a young person in their Sunday-school class or a member of their Bible-study group for whom they have been praying and pleading with God responds in tears to God's call to turn to Christ and calls out to him as the all-sufficient Saviour.

The most famous of all speeches made by Martin Luther

King had as its recurring theme the phrase 'I have a dream'. As God's people—those who are seeking to serve God—what is our dream for that part of God's kingdom in which he has placed us?

EZRA: THE MAIN EVENT

It has been my privilege and joy to see God at work in people's lives, both in salvation and also in restoration to his ways; but such work has tended to be quiet and progressive rather than sudden and dramatic. When we come to Ezra, however, there was a time when God's work in the lives of the people God called him to serve was both very open and very dramatic. One incident clearly and unquestionably demonstrates that God was at work through Ezra's ministry. The only slightly unexpected thing is that this incident is not recorded in the book that bears Ezra's name; instead it is to be found in Nehemiah 8–10 (we will look at these chapters in more detail later). The foundations for what happens in Nehemiah 8 are laid in the key things that we learn about Ezra in the book of Ezra itself (more on that later). And there is one key quality above all others which forms the bedrock of what happens in that chapter.

Ezra is shown to us clearly to be a man of God's Word (Neh. 8:1, 3, 5—8). He, above all others, could be trusted to bring God's Word before the people of God, to read it (and care enough to read it aloud for three or four hours), to value it (v. 6) and then, with the others alongside him that day, to make clear to the people what God was saying to his people from that same Word.

We can see something of the clarity of what was brought

before the people from the Word of God from the way in which those same people were able to respond to what they had heard. So, for example, they could in detail recount the history of God's dealings, God's purposes and God's call on the lives of his people and then the way in which their forefathers had failed time and again. A recounting of this is set out in the confession in Nehemiah 9.

EZRA: SUPPLEMENT TO THE MAIN EVENT

But this day was far more than just a time of teaching leading to a SAT for the people to sit (not a Scholastic Assessment Text but a Spiritual Acknowledgement Test). As Ezra faithfully and fully completed the task which the people called on him to carry out, there was a response to God's Word which went far beyond intellectual assent (agreement at head level); here was heartfelt acquiescence (the response of overwhelmed hearts to the overflowing certainty of their, their parents' and their grandparents' rebellion against God, their guilt as stubborn and hard-hearted rejecters of God's love, and God's glorious care for them). That response is seen in their tears, the weeping and the mourning we find in verse 9.

But that weeping was turned into work: the making of a new covenant with God (Neh. 9–10). The people were moved to go away and do something about what they had heard.

What we see through Ezra was a work of God which had a powerful effect on the people of God: a work that affected their emotions, their wills, their desires and their actions. This was more than a momentary smarting of the tear ducts; this was something that would transform people drawn from many places and with many different experiences and bring them together with the clear and common purpose of walking in God's ways as best they could.

Was this work of God a revival? I recommend Brian Edwards' excellent book *Revival: A People Saturated with God*,[2] which may help you to answer this question.

The people on that day were not involved in discussion and debate—even on such weighty matters as the exact nature of what was happening to them. For them, what was clear was that God was at work, that God was using this man in the simple explanation of God's Word. All that mattered was that they made the right response to the God who was so clearly active in their midst.

OUR DREAM

As we move forward into New Testament days, what mattered for Paul, who was formerly known as Saul, was what God had done for him, and then how he should respond to God—as a saved sinner, appointed apostle and someone gripped by the power and wonder of the gospel (God's good news in and through the person of Jesus Christ).

It was God in the person of Jesus Christ who met with Paul on the road to Damascus. That meeting defined Paul for the rest of his life (Acts 9:1–19). Even when he was thrown into prison in Philippi, he could sing praise to God from his prison cell because of that defining change that had taken place in his life (Acts 16:16–34). When he was brought face to face with the evidence of comparative religion while walking through Athens, his response was defined by his knowing and being known by the one true God (Acts 17:16–34).

As we look further at the life of Ezra we will be able to see something of the way in which God brought him to the point where he could be used as he was in the events recorded in Nehemiah 8. Before we continue, though, we need to ask ourselves some questions. What makes us who we are? What underpins, motivates and defines our lives, actions, hopes and dreams? Are we like Paul, who could say to the Galatian church, 'I no longer live, but Christ lives in me. The life I live in the body, I live by faith in the Son of God, who loved me and gave himself for me' (Gal. 2:20)?

An English pastor once visited a country in South-East Asia with two members from his church. On one of the Sundays of their visit they were invited to provide the preacher at the largest Baptist church in that country's second city. Although the pastor was himself a faithful and godly preacher, he graciously offered the opportunity to one of his companions that morning. The man concerned had not preached often and was nervous of the responsibility given to him. At the end of the message, about ten men ran down the church towards the pulpit, initially causing consternation and concern. However, once the confusion had died down and the men were questioned, it became clear that, independently of one another, these men were moved by God through what they had heard and wanted to ask God for forgiveness and to seek salvation in and through the Lord Jesus Christ.

Nothing like this had happened in the pastor's previous visit to that country—nor had he ever known it in his ministry in the UK. What a joy it would be if God were so to move hearts and minds powerfully and frequently when God's servants faithfully minister God's Word—whether in the UK, US or other places around the world!

A DEFINING MOMENT

Clear, defining moments occurred in the lives of many of the characters to whom we are introduced in the New Testament.

PAUL

We have already thought about Paul and his being arrested by Jesus Christ while on the road to Damascus. We saw how for Paul, that moment became the foundation for the rest of his life. He acknowledged this openly (for example, before the crowd in Jerusalem in Acts 22 and before Agrippa in Acts 26) and he also wrote about it in his letters (one of the most powerful examples being 1 Tim. 1:12–16).

For Paul, his meeting with Jesus was a unique moment that changed him for ever.

THOMAS

But what about Thomas? The most wonderful expression of a life-changing meeting with the risen Lord Jesus Christ is Thomas's powerful and profound phrase 'My Lord and my God!' (John 20:28). John uses these words to lead into a summary of his whole Gospel, ending with the challenge for his readers to respond, like Thomas, by believing that Jesus is the Christ, the Son of God; for it is 'by believing [that] you may have life in his name' (John 20:31).

Yet for many, if not most, of us, Thomas is best known as 'doubting Thomas': a man who lacked faith, who would not believe what the other apostles told him, and who would only proceed on the basis of hard, physical evidence. What a shame that the man who made such a powerful declaration of belief is so often remembered for an apparent failure to believe as he should!

PETER

When we come to consider Peter, what moments defined him?

- Being enabled by God to confess Jesus as 'the Christ, the Son of the living God' (Matt. 16:16)
- Denying Jesus (Matt. 26:69–75)
- Being forgiven by Christ (John 21)
- Preaching at Pentecost about Christ's crucifixion and resurrection (Acts 2:36)
- Opening the door of the gospel to the Gentiles (Acts 10) or being complicit in trying to wedge it shut against them (Gal. 2:11–12)
- Warmly commending that same Paul who had opposed him (2 Peter 3:15–16)

US

What moment or moments define us for who we are today and who we hope to be in the days that lie ahead until we enter eternity?

One of the sadnesses of my teenage years was that, while I went to church, read my Bible, and was active in some aspects of Christian work and witness, no one had drawn my attention to the key event which Jesus Christ himself said to Nicodemus 'must' happen (John 3:7; see also vv. 3, 5). No one had told me that unless I was born again (converted) I would never see the kingdom of God.

Do you know what it is to be born again? Does that event define your life? Is that certainty and confidence the one key event which marks out your life, compared with which all other factors relating to education, employment, family and friendships are secondary?

For some, being born again may be encapsulated in a moment, while the experience for others is like that of the man in John 9 who could simply look back and say, 'I was blind but now I see!' (v. 25). Whatever the actual circumstances of our entering a new life in Christ, to become new people in Christ we must be born again. Are you?

FOR FURTHER STUDY

1. What examples can you think of where God is shown to be working out his purposes against apparently overwhelming odds in either the Old or the New Testament?

2. How did God make it clear in those situations—and in some of the incidents already mentioned in this book—that he remains the one with sovereign power?

3. What did the arrogant emperor Nebuchadnezzar acknowledge when his sanity was restored (see Dan. 4:34–37)?

TO THINK ABOUT AND DISCUSS

1. Martin Luther King said, 'I have a dream today.' What dream or dreams do you have—for yourself, your family members, your church, for the specific area(s) of Christian service with which you are involved?

2. What are the foundations in which your dreams, hopes and ambitions are rooted? How might a rereading of Colossians 2:6–7 affect your answers to these questions?

3. Do you know Jesus Christ? If so, what changes has knowing him made to your life?

4. Ezra was entrusted with the task of reading and giving the *meaning of God's Word. Which things or people have helped you gain a clearer understanding of the meaning of God's Word?*

Notes

1 Charles Schultz, *Nobody's Perfect, Charlie Brown* (London: Coronet Books, 1973) (no page).
2 Brian Edwards, *Revival: A People Saturated with God* (Darlington: Evangelical Press, 1990).

3 An empty place waiting

(Ezra 1–6)

HE'S BEHIND YOU!

In the UK we are familiar with a longstanding and well-established form of entertainment that is normally reserved for the period just after Christmas: the pantomime. Within a pantomime are a number of well-used slapstick routines and examples of verbal gymnastics. So ingrained are they within the pantomime tradition that an audience would leave the theatre feeling cheated if they hadn't been required to sit through certain sequences.

One sequence involves an argument between two characters—an argument in which the audience are invited to join in order to assist one side or the other on the basis of either 'Oh no he didn't!' or 'Oh yes he did!' Another is the arrival either of a comic character (such as a pantomime cow or horse) or of the baddy ('Boo'/'Hiss'), whose appearance is plainly obvious to everyone except the hero or heroine standing centre stage. The audience is invited to be involved in warning the key character by shouting out, 'He's/It's behind you!'

A well-rehearsed and choreographed group of actors can keep up for many minutes the illusion that the 'unseen' character remains unheard and unknown, as they move and dance around one another on the stage. Then, of course, the joke can be played again later in the performance—with the audience still fully engaged with the action.

The fact that the book of Ezra is named after a person suggests that Ezra was a key player in the events revealed to us by God. Yet for six of the ten chapters in the book, Ezra himself is not mentioned: nothing is heard or spoken of him at all. He is, as it were, standing in the wings of the story—waiting for the time when God will reveal him and place him at the heart of all that he is doing for his people at this point in their history. So, while the other characters and events take place oblivious of Ezra and (much more significantly) apparently ignorant of God at work, our hearts, if not our mouths, should be screaming out, 'He's behind you!'

In the next chapter we will look at some of the ways God involved himself with the people, but in this chapter our focus needs to be on Ezra himself.

IT'S PREPARATION—BUT NOT AS WE KNOW IT

While we are not told this specifically, it is clear from the way in which Ezra steps onto the stage fully formed and equipped for the work that God had for him to do that in this period covered by chapters 1–6 Ezra was being prepared by God. But this preparation was not a series of rehearsals for a part in a dramatic production; Ezra was to be a real person whom God would use in a real situation at a real point in history. For him to be that person took far more than face paint and a well-tailored costume. It involved a lifetime of preparation and the sovereign and merciful hand of God on his life.

QUESTIONS, QUESTIONS

We are not told very much about Ezra's personal life. There are many questions we could ask about him and his background:

- Was he one of the prize Jewish youths carried off to Babylon with Daniel and his friends (Dan. 1:3–4)? Unless Ezra is very old when we first meet him, it is likely that he was taken into captivity later or even born in captivity.[1] His father, Seraiah (Ezra 7:1[2]), the chief priest, was taken away among the last wave of captives following the final overthrow of Jerusalem (2 Kings 25:18).
- Did he have an established role around the great king's table, as Nehemiah did (Neh. 1:11)? Or was he someone who lived outside the palace walls, like Mordecai (Esth. 2:19–23)? He was certainly known well enough within the Persian hierarchy to have been specifically named in a letter from the emperor (Ezra 7:12).
- We know a little of his family background (Ezra 7:1–5), but exactly what training had he received? Did he receive it solely in the land of exile, or had he already been able to travel to and from Jerusalem (as Nehemiah's family did—Neh. 1)? In whatever way that training had come about, it had developed a particular quality in Ezra (that of a teacher) which would be noticed by his human governors and also, more importantly, by God himself (7:12, 6).

A DARK BACKGROUND

While we know little of Ezra's personal background, we know quite a lot about the events which had been taking place both in the land of Israel and also in the wider world dominated by the empires of Babylon and then Persia. For the people of God it was, in many ways, a time of disaster and despair because the land which since Abraham's day had been foundational to their special relationship with God had been conquered, and the people had been carried far away from the place where God's presence was to be known—the temple in Jerusalem. And yet, as can be seen in chapters 1–3, something was stirring and some of the people had started returning to the land and had begun to rebuild that temple. But those green shoots of promise were, it might have appeared to those living through those days, nipped in the bud by opposition and unfairness (and also some inept government; see 4:6–23), culminating in a full stop (4:24).

So Ezra was a man who had grown up among a people scarred by disaster and seasoned with disappointment. Despite being born into the family of the high priest, a family that would have given generations of service to God (as all priests came from a specific part of the tribe of Levi), Ezra appeared to have little or nothing to give him or his family the hope that God had promised through Jeremiah (Jer. 29:10–11).

However, Ezra was a man who was being prepared by God, in God's good purposes, for a great work for God and God's people, even though there was nothing to be said about Ezra in chapters 1–6.

NOT JUST FOR EZRA

We are in a similar situation. The Bible tells us—those who are now, or who will one day become, God's children—that we have been loved by God since before the foundation of the world (see, for example, Eph. 1:4). We are loved with an everlasting love that will, in God's good and perfect timing, fit us to stand before his throne in heaven and to enjoy an eternity of glory with him and all his redeemed people (or, as one of our wonderful Christmas carols says, Jesus came to 'fit us for heaven to live with [him] there'³).

While we are on our way there, God has prepared good works for us to do (Eph. 2:10)—things that are pleasing to God and of positive worth in this world. And these good things both require us to be prepared to do them—just as David's preparation as a shepherd boy enabled him to defeat Goliath (1 Sam. 17:34–36)—and are themselves a preparation for what God has in store for us in the future. In the life of Daniel, for example, each step of his obedience to God led to a greater trust in God, and enabled him and his friends to trust, pray to and obey God in new ways which, in turn, were means of giving testimony about the God they worshipped to the emperors they served.

All the way my Saviour leads me;
What have I to ask beside?
Can I doubt His tender mercy,
Who through life has been my Guide?
Heav'nly peace, divinest comfort,
Here by faith in Him to dwell!
For I know, whate'er befall me,
Jesus doeth all things well;   (Fanny J. Crosby, 1875)

PREPARATION

In the New Testament, we read of other people whose lives were clearly marked by a time of preparation before a period of service. In the case of Timothy, for example, Paul could point to generations of faithful (and faith-full) family members who had encouraged Timothy in his work of proclaiming the unique gospel of salvation in and through Jesus Christ.

Paul himself could speak of aspects of his life that had prepared him for the work that God had planned for him. In his spiritual life, his training under Gamaliel had given him a clear and incisive appreciation of the Old Testament—which 'only' required the enlightening work of God the Holy Spirit to allow him to see how everything pointed to Jesus as the Christ, the one Mediator between God and man. His practical skills as a tent-maker were used to great effect in Corinth in the discipling and training of Aquila and Priscilla.

However, Paul was acutely aware that relying on those foundations would never be enough. There was something—indeed, Someone—who was of surpassingly greater worth than any of these experiences, and compared with whom they were actually like a pile of stinking rubbish. For, as Peter put it, 'salvation is found in no one else'; it is only in Christ's name that 'we must be saved' (Acts 4:12).

You may be reading this book because you have had good and positive foundations laid in your life, such as the recognition of the value of God's Word and of all the characters revealed to us in it (even those as apparently peripheral as Ezra). Yet those foundations are not enough if you are not yet in Christ and do not have God's gift of eternal life.

There may have been circumstances in your life which, with the benefit of hindsight, you can see have been used to shape you into the person you are now. Has that shaping been part of God's work in you to prepare you to be with him and his Son in glory for all eternity?

Or you may be in the middle of a situation that is all but overwhelming you. Are you able, with God's help, to recognize that, whatever circumstance you find yourself in, Christ remains Immanuel (God with you), as he promised (Heb. 13:5–6), in and through the working of God the Holy Spirit?

FOR FURTHER STUDY

1. David, the shepherd boy; a captive slave girl in the household of a leprous general; Peter, the blustering and impetuous fisherman; and Paul, a would-be murderer: are these likely or unlikely instruments for God to use?

2. Look at the lives of the women mentioned in Matthew 1. What strikes you about the purity, holiness and blamelessness of their lives?

3. How did God, either directly or indirectly, have to challenge and encourage men like Jeremiah (Jer. 1) and Timothy (1 Tim. 4:12; 5:21–23; 2 Tim. 1:6–7)?

TO THINK ABOUT AND DISCUSS

1. We all have different backgrounds and experiences. As you look back, what key events have shaped your life in general, and are they the same events that have had an impact on your spiritual life?

2. Are there areas/events in your life that you find difficult to deal with? How should you respond to them? Jeremiah, for example, was quite free in acknowledging such events to God (e.g. Jer. 20:7–8). What will help you to recognize and remember God's good and gracious hand behind these events? (See Ezra 7:9; 8:18; Neh. 2:8.)

3. Are there things that God has for you to do at this point in your life which are different from those you knew you should do some years ago? These might be in terms of work- or family-based roles, roles within your local church or other Christian activities. Do you regret or rejoice in the changes? Why?

4. The future is in God's hands, but do you see any clues in what has been happening in your life recently that might indicate what lies ahead for you in his service?

Notes

1   The exile lasted seventy years, from a little before 600 BC to around 540 BC. So if Ezra had gone into exile at the very beginning he would have been elderly when he returned to Jerusalem.

2   The Bible sometimes uses the term 'father' to mean remote ancestor. Seraiah is also recorded as being the grandfather of Jeshua, another character we will meet in our next chapter, who returned to Jerusalem some years before Ezra. (Seraiah was the father of Jozadak (also known as Jehozadak; 1 Chr. 6:14) and Jeshua (or Joshua, as he is known in Haggai and Zechariah) was Jehozadak's son (e.g. Hag. 1:1).) Was Ezra Jeshua's uncle, or did they have another relationship within Seraiah's family?

3   **John T. McFarland** (1851–1913), v. 3 of 'Away in a Manger'.

4 The other side of the coin

(Ezra 3:1–2; 5:1–2; Hag. 1; Zech. 3)

HEADS AND TAILS

I have never seen any, but I have heard that some coins are double-headed—that is, rather than having heads and tails (or, more technically, obverse and reverse), they have heads on both sides. For those who are desperate to win when tossing a coin, the knowledge that the coin is doubled-headed is a great advantage. But for every other purpose—paying for shopping, using a coin-operated vending machine or even for some basic investigation into probability theory—a double-headed coin is of no use whatsoever.

As we continue to look at the opening chapters in Ezra we see the 'obverse' to Ezra's story. Four names mentioned at the beginning of chapters 3 and 5 remind us that in God's plans and purposes it was not just Ezra who was being prepared for what lay ahead. God was also preparing the people by providing prophets to speak to them on his behalf and leaders who would act as trail-blazers in walking in God's ways.

Who were these four people? In the book of Ezra itself we are given little more than their names and, in some cases, their roles:

- Zerubbabel (3:2; 5:2)
- Jeshua (called Joshua in the books of Haggai and Zechariah)—identified as one of the priests (3:2; 5:2)
- Haggai and Zechariah—prophets (5:1)

However, if we turn to the books in the Bible bearing the names of Haggai and Zechariah we can find out a number of key things about these men and their place in God's purposes.

KEY ROLES

Zerubbabel and Jeshua were not simply two leaders among others: Jeshua was the high priest and Zerubbabel was the governor (Hag. 1:1; Zech. 3:1). Between them they held the positions of highest authority and greatest responsibility, both spiritually and politically, in the province of Judah, under the sovereignty of the emperor in Susa.

The role of governor was an imperial appointment (we see that when the emperor later appoints Nehemiah to that same role—Neh. 5:14). But far more than just an imperial appointee, Zerubbabel was God's man for the job and part of God's eternal purposes, not only for the people and the land of Judah, but for the whole world.

Zerubbabel was, in many ways, the most unlikely of imperial appointees. The last semi-independent king of Judah had demonstrated a rebellious streak requiring an overwhelming response from his Babylonian masters (2 Chr. 36:11–14; Jer. 52:3–15). If there was any chance that this was a family trait, imperial prudence would surely have dictated that future appointments would have little if any connection to the royal house that had once ruled the land. We would think that men suitable for the role of governor would be those whose ambition was limited and who recognized that their role was solely an imperial gift: men who could, therefore, be counted on to remain loyal to the empire.[1]

But Zerubbabel was a direct descendant of David and Solomon—and, far more wonderfully, also an ancestor of 'great David's greater Son'[2] (Matt. 1:12–13). Here was a man who stood at the centre of God's eternal purposes and, as part of those eternal purposes, was appointed to govern the land and lead the people in the days that led up to Ezra's arrival in Jerusalem.

JESHUA'S NEW CLOTHES

It was not so much who he was as what had happened to him that made Jeshua the man of God's provision for his people.

In Ezra we are told of his parentage: he was the son of Jozadak (called Jehozadak in Zech. 3). And Jozadak's father was Seraiah (1 Chr. 6:14), who had been chief priest at the time of the first captivity, when Nebuchadnezzar had carried off a great many people from Jerusalem to Babylon (1 Chr. 6:14–15; 2 Kings 25:18).

What mattered more than anything, though, was that Jeshua was a man who knew what it was to be forgiven by God. This was something that God saw fit to put in the public domain through the writings of Zechariah—specifically in Zechariah 3.

We are not told exactly what it was that Jeshua had done that had brought him to the position in which he is found at the beginning of Zechariah 3. However, there is no doubt that the filthy rags Jeshua wore (v. 3) reflected his standing before God. They were more than simply a reminder that even the best things we can do are like filthy rags in God's sight (Isa. 64:6). When Satan stood before God to accuse Jeshua, there was accuracy in his accusations.

But the 'angel of the LORD'³ would have none of it, and instead of being accused, Jeshua was forgiven; instead of the filthy rags he deserved, he was given a rich garment to wear and a clean turban for his head (vv. 4–5).

God had raised up a leader who knew the joy of God's undeserved forgiveness and the wonder of restoration to God's service. Not that the restoration was without its challenges; God gave Jeshua a high calling (v. 7). It is never less. But God's leader was indeed a 'brand plucked from the fire' (v. 2, ESV), and one who would lead God's people with his feet planted on that sure foundation.

CALL AND RESPONSE

Alongside Zerubbabel and Jeshua God also gave the people prophets, whose specific role was to stir the hearts of the people to action with words of both challenge and encouragement. Haggai was direct when God said through him, 'This is what the LORD Almighty says: These people say, "The time has not yet come for the LORD's house to be built" … Is it a time for you yourselves to be living in your panelled houses, while this house remains a ruin?' (Hag. 1:2, 4).

This was God's message to a people who, in his loving care, had returned from exile. They had seen God's promises through Jeremiah start to come true with tangible reality in their lives, but the promises were only partly fulfilled. Work on the temple had started, but in the face of opposition it had ground to a halt and the focus of attention had moved from the purposes of God to their own ends, from God's house to their own homes.

However they tried to justify it, these people were disobeying God and rejecting the very reason and purpose for which God had enabled them to go back to the land: namely, to rebuild the temple and renew the covenant relationship between themselves and God. And it was the role of the prophets to hold a mirror before the eyes of the people so that they could clearly see how far they had strayed from the place where God commanded them to be.

The book of Haggai records how, as the people listened to the prophets, they responded immediately: 'So the LORD stirred up the spirit of Zerubbabel son of Shealtiel, governor of Judah, and the spirit of Joshua son of Jehozadak, the high priest, and the spirit of the whole remnant of the people. They came and began to work on the house of the LORD Almighty, their God' (Hag. 1:14).

BLESSING

As a result of that obedience blessing flowed from God, as we see, for example, in Haggai 2:19. This blessing had within it the hope of more glorious blessings to follow (Hag. 2:22–23; Zech. 8:1–5; 9:9–11).

But—and there was a clear 'but' for the people living in Jerusalem when Ezra travelled there from Babylon—those promised blessings remained clearly linked to the people's ongoing response to God's call on their lives, a response that would come from their hearts and be seen in their actions: 'This is what the LORD Almighty says: "Administer true justice; show mercy and compassion to one another. Do not oppress the widow or the fatherless, the alien or the poor. In your hearts do not think evil of each other"' (Zech. 7:9–10).

FULFILMENT

So far in Ezra we have seen three roles: the high priest, prophets and the governor (leader/ruler/king). The New Testament presents to us, centre stage, one supremely able and glorious person in whom all three roles were perfectly fused: the Lord Jesus Christ.

From the early days of the Old Testament, God spoke, either directly or through his appointed leaders, of one who would come as Prophet, Priest and King. For example:

- Moses spoke of a *prophet* who would one day be raised up by God (Deut. 18:15).
- The priest Melchizedek made a very brief appearance in Genesis 14:18–20, but the psalmist referred to him, saying that one day another *priest* in his order would come; this priest would be eternal (Ps. 110:4). This was recognized by the writer of the letter to the Hebrews as being fulfilled in Christ (Heb. 7:17).
- Through Nathan and Ezekiel, God promised a *king* in David's line, one whose kingdom would be eternal (1 Chr. 17:11–15; Ezek. 37:24–28).

In case we doubt that these roles all find their focus in Jesus Christ, we need look no further than the list of names in Matthew 1 (where Zerubbabel's name appears in vv. 12–13). Here we find the name Jesus, which is a variation of the name Joshua/Jeshua (and vice versa), which means 'the Lord is Salvation'.

In the Old Testament, those who held the positions of prophet, priest and king were all anointed. This demonstrated that God's presence, authority and power rested on them: they could speak for God, stand as mediator between God and his people, and rule God's people in his name and for his glory. For example:

- Elijah was sent to anoint Elisha as prophet after him (1 Kings 19:16).
- Aaron and his sons were to be anointed and consecrated as priests (Exod. 30:30).
- Samuel was sent to the house of Jesse to anoint David as king over Israel (1 Sam. 16:1, 13).

Likewise, Isaiah promised that the Messiah would be anointed by God:

The Spirit of the Sovereign LORD is on me,
  because the LORD has anointed me
  to preach good news to the poor.
He has sent me to bind up the broken-hearted,
  to proclaim freedom for the captives
  and release from darkness for the prisoners,
to proclaim the year of the LORD's favour
  and the day of vengeance of our God,
to comfort all who mourn ...   (Isa. 61:1–2)

It was this promise that Jesus read out in the synagogue in his home town of Nazareth, declaring that it had been fulfilled in him (Luke 4:21). The people did not acknowledge him as the Christ (the Greek word translated 'anointed one' is *kristos*, or Christ), instead choosing to reject him.

Christ's claim is unique in the world and among all other religions. Some religions claim that their founder spoke for God or, for example, had great understanding of the purpose of pain and suffering in this world. But only Jesus makes the claim that he is God's anointed prophet, priest and king: that he has authority because he is God himself incarnate among us, our Immanuel.

How do you respond to that claim? C. S. Lewis made a trenchant comment:

I am trying here to prevent anyone saying the really foolish thing that people often say about Him: I'm ready to accept Jesus as a great moral teacher, but I don't accept his claim to be God. That is the one thing we must not say. A man who was merely a man and said the sort of things Jesus said would not be a great moral teacher. He would either be a lunatic—on the level with the man who says he is a poached egg—or else he would be the Devil of Hell. You must make your choice. Either this man was, and is, the Son of God, or else a madman or something worse. You can shut him up for a fool, you can spit at him and kill him as a demon or you can fall at his feet and call him Lord and God, but let us not come with any patronizing nonsense about his being a great human teacher. He has not left that open to us. He did not intend to.4

I think it is fair to say that we can be reasonably sure on which side of the line C. S. Lewis stood. What about you?

FOR FURTHER STUDY

1. Why did the people in Ezra's day need the leaders that God provided for them?

2. If you have not done so already, read the story of Jeshua (Joshua) in Zechariah 3. Which specific parts of the story are encouragements to you, and why?

3. When Jesus asked the disciples, 'Who do the crowds say I am?' (Luke 9:18), the response gave a very accurate reflection of people's views at the time (v. 19; compare vv. 7–8). What do people say about Jesus today? How different are those views from those of C. S. Lewis's day?

TO THINK ABOUT AND DISCUSS

1. What can help us gain a greater understanding of who Jesus truly is?

2. As your understanding of Jesus increases, do you find that there are changes in your response to things that are said about him which conflict with who he truly is? Give examples.

3. How can you communicate your responses to such views in ways which are honouring to Jesus himself?

Notes

1 For an example of such a man appointed in Jeremiah's day, see Jeremiah 40.

2 **James Montgomery,** 'Hail to the Lord's Anointed', 1821.

3 I would understand this to be a pre-incarnate appearance of the Lord Jesus Christ. See **Jonathan Stephen's** book *Theophany: Close Encounters with the Son of God* (Epsom: Day One, 1998), which introduces us to the idea of theophany or Christophany.

4 **C. S. Lewis,** *Mere Christianity* (London: Fount, 1977), (no page).

5 Have Bible, will travel

(Ezra 7:1–12)

ARE WE NEARLY THERE YET?

What is the longest journey you have ever made? I remember the first time I drove to Cornwall from central-southern England: it took nearly a whole day to get there. Today, on a good day, with reasonable traffic conditions, that journey would take half the time.

When I was a child, my family was posted to the great port city of Singapore. By boat, it took us over two weeks to travel there from the UK. Today, a direct flight is measured in hours, not days or weeks.

Perhaps you have memories of journeys when you or your children called out with impatience, 'Are we nearly there yet?'

In Ezra 7:1–12 God tells us of the journey which Ezra made from Babylon to Jerusalem—a journey measured not in hours, days or even weeks, but in months. It took four whole months (from the first day of the first month to the first day of the fifth month)—and that was only because God had been good to him on the journey (v. 9). How long the journey would have been if God had not been gracious to him is beyond our ken.

WHY BOTHER?

Why does God bother to record the length of the journey?

What purpose does a record of this journey have—a journey that took longer than any journey the vast majority of us would ever contemplate yet which, to the people of Ezra's day, was clearly seen as a mark of God's care, concern and favour?

As is so often the case in the Bible, a small and apparently insignificant word, 'For', is key. We are told that this happened '*For* Ezra had devoted himself to the study and observance of the Law of the LORD, and to teaching its decrees and laws in Israel' (v. 10, emphasis added). From the other verses in this section we discover that Ezra was:

- A teacher well versed in the Law of Moses (v. 6)
- Devoted to the study and observance of the Law of the Lord (v. 10)
- Learned in matters concerning the commands and decrees of the Lord (v. 11)
- A teacher of the Law of the God of heaven (v. 12)

In other words, Ezra was a man of God's Word.

THE POWER OF THREE

I remember many years ago a retired engineer explaining in some detail the inherent stability and, hence, the importance of three-sided structures. He did this by pointing to the roof area of the building in which he and those listening to him had gathered. This roof had a lattice-work of triangular-shaped structures made up of rafters and trusses. It was these triangular forms that gave stability and security to the roof.

In Ezra's life, we find in verse 10 that there were three things to which Ezra devoted himself, each of which was directly related to the 'Law of the LORD'.[1]

STUDY

Firstly, Ezra was a man who devoted himself to *studying* the Law of the Lord. 'Study' is a word that does not immediately warm the cockles of my heart. I find it easier to identify with 'the Preacher' when he says that 'much study is a weariness of the flesh' (Eccles. 12:12, ESV).

But Ezra was a man with a very different perspective: he devoted himself to study, but not study as an abstract concept. He was not—at least, not on the face of verse 10—a polymath, someone who has a wide-ranging and eclectic set of interests. Rather, Ezra's study was directed, and it focused on the Law of the Lord.

There were negative and positive reasons for such an all-consuming devotion. From a negative perspective, the prophets (including those who had spoken before the time of exile) made it clear that it was because the people of God had rejected the Law of the Lord and had refused to listen to the Lord that the destruction had come upon them (see Isa. 5:24; Amos 2:4; Jer. 8:8; 2 Chr. 36:15–16).

But, on the positive side, God had promised blessings, both general and specific, to those who delighted and walked in his Law (Ps. 1:2; 119:1; 19:7–10; these psalms would have been very familiar to Ezra, the son of the high priest).

It is a good thing to memorize God's Law, but study is much more than that. In study we gain an understanding of the great themes and purposes in God's Law; we see how God deals with people—both the heroes and the heroines of faith, and those whose lives demonstrate God's mercy and compassion.

OUT FROM THE STUDY

Ezra's study was never intended to be purely a means of acquiring knowledge and information. Nor was it something which was to be reserved for the private world of his personal devotions, his intimate time with God. So, secondly, the understanding he gained of God's Law was to be *applied* to his own life. Some people say that 'Those who can't do, teach', but for Ezra that would have been a totally alien concept. He spent time with God, through studying God's Law, so that he would know God and his purposes and so that his life could be moulded and shaped to fit those purposes.

This should be the desire of each one of God's people. An internal understanding of God's Word (within our minds) should lead to external application, something that is worked out day by day in the way we behave and deal with the people and situations we come into contact with in our homes, places of work and at church.

THOSE WHO CAN, TEACH

For Ezra it went one step further: he, thirdly, also had both the privilege and the awesome responsibility of *teaching* these decrees and laws to God's people, the people of Israel.

James reminds his readers that the role of a teacher of God's Word is one of great responsibility: 'Not many of you should presume to be teachers, my brothers, because you know that we who teach will be judged more strictly' (James 3:1, which introduces teaching for all God's people about the way we all use our words). Yet, having grown up in a home with an equally high and heavy responsibility, Ezra was not discouraged and did not seek a less demanding role: he devoted himself to being a teacher just as much as to study and observe the Law of the Lord.

DEVOTION

Ezra's devotion is like a window into his heart, his passions and his priorities in life. Some people consider that Cliff Richard used to sing of a type of music that 'gets into your heart and soul'. For Ezra, though, it was not music that had that effect on him. It was the Law of the Lord and, through knowing that Law, knowing the Lord of the Law; it was this that infused every fibre of his being and took hold of his life.

Nothing was more precious to him. Nothing had a higher place in his affections. Nothing mattered more to him than the blessings, the joy and the wonder that came through knowing—and being known by—the One who had revealed himself and his purposes through his Law.

BE BEREAN

Paul, when writing to the young pastor Timothy, reminded him of the five-fold value of God's Word in his ministry: '… from infancy you have know the holy Scriptures, which are able to make you wise for salvation through faith in Christ Jesus. All Scripture is God-breathed and is useful for teaching, rebuking, correcting and training in righteousness, so that the man of God may be thoroughly equipped for every good work' (2 Tim. 3:15–16)

You could picture it like this. Think of someone's hand holding a Bible. Underneath is the certainty (the opposable thumb) that it is through the Bible that people are made wise for salvation through faith in Jesus Christ. On top are the four fingers that remind us that the Bible is profitable for:

- Teaching—showing us what is right
- Rebuking—showing us how we have gone wrong
- Correcting—showing us how to get back to what is right
- Training in righteousness—showing us how to keep on doing more and more of what is right

The purpose of this is that the person who is God's and is seeking to do God's will can be equipped 'for every good work'.

This mention of good works reminds us of:

- The purpose of Christ's coming and the salvation that he brought: to make for himself a people eager to do what is good (Titus 2:14)
- The outworking of grace through faith in the lives of believers: people who are created in Christ for good works (Eph. 2:10)
- The glory that goes to God from the good works of his people (Matt. 5:16)

Remember that good works are a response to the great work of Christ in bringing salvation; they are not a means of earning salvation.

It is God's Word that equips us to live the life that God intended us to live, as his people in Christ. Just a few centuries ago, men and women in Europe gave their lives to make it possible for people to be able to have the Bible in their own languages. Today, in the UK, we can nip into our local bookshop and pick up one of a number of translations. If we look on the Internet, the choices available are mind-boggling. But the number of Bibles available does not mean that we are making good use of the treasure that the Bible is.

It is sad to visit the homes of those who are not actively

involved in church life but who may once have been part of a Sunday school class when young. Often such people were awarded Bibles or New Testaments as prizes and those Bibles remain in their homes, gathering dust rather than giving light to hearts and lives. But before we feel smug or self-satisfied, what are we going to do with God's Word? Ezra had his three-fold approach—to study, apply and teach. Some organizations suggest additional methods of making the most of the Bible.[2]

Ezra's approach is good because it involves our understanding, our actions and also our responsibilities to others. It is a reminder that God's Word in our lives is to be far more than just head knowledge or even a heartfelt assent to what God says in it. If we are truly making the most of God's Word, it will affect who we are, what we do and our relationships and dealings with others.

One of the most highly commended groups of people we read about in the book of Acts was the Bereans. Every day they listened to Paul—the man appointed by God to be the apostle to the Gentile (non-Jewish) world—and they went away 'with great eagerness' to study the Scriptures to see if what Paul had said was correct (Acts 17:11). Be a Berean and check out the second half of Luke 10:37.

FOR FURTHER STUDY

1. What words or phrases in the Bible show the many ways of receiving, and helping others to receive, God's Word? (Ps. 119 is a good place to start looking, but, despite its length, it is by no means exhaustive.)

2. Galatians 1:15–18, taken together with Acts 9:24–26, indicates that there was a significant period of time between Paul leaving Damascus and arriving in Jerusalem. It seems that he spent this early period of his Christian life alone with God. We may not be able to spend years in seclusion with God studying his Word, but how can we make getting to know and understand God better through his Word a priority in our lives?

3. Give examples of situations in the Bible where a study of God's Word moved God's people (or a specific person) to action. (Daniel's prayer in Dan. 9 and a young Old Testament king called Josiah would be two examples.)

4. How does Paul—whose own life was shaped by his knowledge of God through God's Word—suggest that the people of God in their lives and living should be moulded by God's purposes as revealed in the Bible? (Think of his instructions in all his letters.)

TO THINK ABOUT AND DISCUSS

1. What difficulties do you experience as you seek to put God's Word into practice in your home and workplace?

2. In Ezra we read of a direct relationship between Ezra's character and God's gracious hand being upon him. Do we always clearly experience that in our lives? When we don't, how do we respond?

3. Do your church leaders encourage you to be Berean in your *listening habits—even if that might result in your questioning or challenging them?*

Notes

1 Are we to understand 'the Law of the LORD' to be a specific reference to the books of the 'Law' (Torah; i.e. the five books of Moses), or a more general description of the Bible as it existed in Ezra's day? The Jewish Old Testament Scriptures (Tanakh) were not yet complete—not least because obviously the events of the books of Ezra and Nehemiah (and their prophet contemporaries) were still unfolding and being recorded at this time. My understanding is that the main emphasis must be on the books of the Law themselves, but as they had been and were coming to be understood through the prophets and other writings (e.g., in the context of Ezra's day, through the prophet Jeremiah).

2 The Navigators (a disciple-making organization) use another hand illustration, one good version of which comes from their group on a US military base. See 'The Hand Illustration', at www.braggnavs.com/The%20Hand.pdf.

6 God's good hand

(Ezra 7:9, 27–28; 8:15–36)

HE OPENED HIS MOUTH AND PUT HIS FOOT RIGHT IN IT

Have you ever said something and immediately wished you could retract your words? Or perhaps you've heard someone else say something that they realized came out wrong, and then watched them try to undo what they said or extricate themselves—which usually ends up making matters worse.

Comedians and comedy scriptwriters make a living by observing and reflecting such verbal calamities. But they can only draw laughter from us because we've been there ourselves. And it is true of Bible characters too. We can picture Thomas, blustering about not believing that Jesus has risen from the dead unless he has tangible proof, and demanding the most outrageous evidence of all—putting his hand into the wound in Jesus's side—with Jesus (theatrically, this is a 'He's behind you!' moment) waiting until Thomas has finished before offering that very proof to him.

Ezra recognized this in himself. Ezra 8:21–23 is a wonderful little expression of honesty: 'I was ashamed to ask the king for soldiers …'—because he'd made a boast about God's power to protect his people. Now Ezra and those who were with him had to live up to that boast. Might there have been one or two in that company who would have preferred

Ezra to have been a little less confident in his interview with the king?

REASONS TO BE WORRIED

Today we live in a world where it is quite usual for people to travel half-way round the world in less than twenty-four hours. My son lived for a time on one of the Hawaiian islands and for nearly half the year we were divided by a time difference of eleven hours. Yet because of this same time difference it would have been possible for us to catch a plane early in the morning from London and be with him in the evening of the same day.

The hours we spend travelling today are mere snippets in comparison with the proposed journey that Ezra and those who travelled with him were to take. We have no real idea how long this journey would normally take, although, as we saw in our last chapter, we do know that with God's good favour it 'only' took four months. And that journey was not through territory known to them, or in places that were always hospitable and welcoming. Much of the journey would have been through dry, dusty and barren land.

Ezra 8:31 hints that there was no guarantee of safe passage either: 'enemies and bandits' might have been encountered along the way. Yes, they were travelling within the borders of the Babylonian empire and with the authority and blessing of the king, but words on a sealed parchment written in the language of the court might not impress brigands from the northern border of the empire who stumbled across Ezra and his party—even if they could read.

That is why the king offered Ezra an armed guard: to ensure that his orders were obeyed by whomever Ezra met in his travels.

EZRA'S CONFIDENCE

But Ezra had confidence in God; or, at the very least, he had made a clear profession of confidence in God to the king and could not now go back on that profession (8:22).

At this point Ezra clearly had a choice. He could go back to the king and ask him for help in the form of soldiers to guard them on their way. Or he could remain true to what he had told the king and look to God himself to provide the support and assistance that they needed for their journey.

Ezra was honest enough to admit that part of the reason for the choice he made was shame at having to admit that he might have been wrong to put his trust in God (8:22). However much a part that played in his decision, it was to God he now turned, and it was in God he placed his trust.

WHAT ABOUT THOSE WITH HIM?

But what about those with him? Wouldn't they have been within their rights to think of Ezra not so much as Ezra the Scribe but as Oliver Hardy, of whom they could say, 'That's another fine mess you've got us into'? The people's response, however, seems to reflect a shared willingness to trust God, a shared commitment to serve God and a shared looking to God alone for help. So 8:23 says that 'we' fasted and petitioned 'our' God; and God answered 'our' prayer.

Ezra recognized that shared dedication to God's service. He reminded the people that it wasn't just the material things which were being transported to help rebuild the temple that were consecrated to God; the people who had given themselves to the work shared that same consecration (8:28).

PROOF OF THE PUDDING

It is sometimes said that words are cheap. It was all very well for Ezra to talk a good talk—whether to the king, those who were to travel with him or even to himself (as he records his thoughts and feelings for us in this book). What was needed was for those words to be translated into action: for the claims to be tested and the journey to begin. This happened on the twelfth day of the first month (8:31).

And … there was nothing special to report. Indeed, all Ezra has to say of the actual journey was that there were no problems: 'The hand of our God was on us, and he protected us from enemies and bandits along the way.' So they arrived in Jerusalem.

Nothing spectacular, nothing dramatic—God simply proved to be utterly and completely trustworthy. Every doubt proved groundless, and any uncertainty was shown to be baseless. Every prayer was answered and God demonstrated that he was more than able to bring them safely to the end of their journey.

RESPONSE

At the end of the journey it was time for:
- Rest (8:32)
- Completion of the work (8:33–36)
- Thanksgiving (8:35)

Whether or not they always come in that order, these three elements will often be found in those whose trust in God brings them through times of trial to a conclusion of the task to which God has called them.

- Work will be brought to a clear and satisfactory conclusion—whether it be the work of salvation in the heart and life of someone whom God has called you to serve, or the equipping of someone for service and ministry in God's kingdom.
- Completed work will lead properly to thanksgiving—thanksgiving to God for what he has done and for his grace and mercy in bringing to fruition his good, pleasing and perfect will.
- There will be a time of rest—whether the periodic times of rest that God has designed for us to enjoy while here on this earth, or the final and eternal rest around his throne in glory.

Using the example of ancient Israel's failure to enter God's promised rest, the writer of the letter to the Hebrews challenged his readers in this way:

Therefore, since the promise of entering his rest still stands, let us be careful that none of you be found to have fallen short of it. For we also have had the gospel preached to us, just as they did; but the message they heard was of no value to them, because those who heard did not combine it with faith ... There remains, then, a Sabbath-rest for the people of God; for anyone who enters God's rest also rests from his own work, just as God did from his. Let us, therefore, make every effort to enter that rest, so that no one will fall by following their example of disobedience. (Heb. 4:1–2, 9–11)

CAN GOD BE TRUSTED?

At some point in our lives—perhaps in a number of different situations—this will be a crucial question.

God calls us to follow him—to follow him in this life, to follow him through death, and to follow him into an eternity of glory before his throne.

Following him in this life may be difficult. For some it will involve difficulties in our relationships with our families. In some places around the world, it can lead to a total destruction of family relationships, but Christ challenged his first disciples to remember that they had to love him more than any human relationship (e.g. Luke 14:26, where his wording is very stark). For some it will involve a change of work or career; for others, a potential life partner may no longer be a possible choice. There may be years of disappointment or uncertainty as our dreams and aspirations for our lives are not fulfilled. None of this is necessarily true for everyone—but it can be true for some, and it might be true for you.

When it comes to the end of our lives, when it becomes clearer that it is 'in Christ alone' that our hope is found, when we reach the door of death and know that there is no one except Christ who has been through that door and returned to report what lies on the other side[1]—the question 'Can we truly rely on God's promises?' needs to be answered with greater clarity and certainty.

In these situations we do well to remember that we have an enemy who prowls around seeking to devour us and our trust in Christ, and who can appear in many guises—whether to strike fear into our hearts (1 Peter 5:8) or to appear as sweetness and light (2 Cor. 11:14).

There cannot be many Christians who have not had, in one form or another, a train of thought which has called into question God's ability to make good on his promises or who have wondered whether it is really worthwhile to put our trust in God when there are so many other things that could be part of our lives. This was the enemy's tactic at the beginning of time (Gen. 3:1), and it was the same tactic that was used on Jesus Christ when he was here on earth (Matt. 4:1–10).

Ezra's example of confidence in God was followed in New Testament days by Peter as he stood before the Sanhedrin. When challenged about his actions and told to be silent, he replied firmly, 'we cannot help speaking about what we have seen and heard' (Acts 4:18–20). That same determination was shown by Martin Luther: 'I cannot choose but adhere to the word of God, which has possession of my conscience; nor can I possibly, nor will I even make any recantation, since it is neither safe nor honest to act contrary to conscience! Here I stand; I cannot do otherwise, so help me God! Amen.'[2]

But while these sterling and glorious statements of faith are, I trust, encouraging and challenging to us, they are, by their very nature, statements of faith which had yet to stand the greatest test: the test of truth. Can God—will God—make his promises come true?

And for the answer to this we can look at clear biblical examples: from Rahab's rescue from Jericho to Daniel's protection in the den of lions; from Joseph's promotion in Pharaoh's court to David's victory over Goliath. But above all others, the one that must be our rock-solid foundation is the death and resurrection of the Lord Jesus Christ.

As he walked with two disciples on the road to Emmaus the

first Easter Sunday morning, Jesus explained to them that 'the Christ [had] to suffer ... and then enter his glory' (Luke 24:26). Just a few hours later he reminded a group of his disciples that the whole of God's Word pointed to the certainty that 'The Christ will suffer and rise from the dead on the third day' (Luke 24:46).

It is in the fulfilment of that promise that we live; it is with the same power used to raise Christ from the dead that our salvation is assured (1 Cor. 6:14); and it is because Christ was raised, is alive and will one day return, just as he promised, that Peter could urge those to whom he wrote to look forward to the end of the journey, when all the promises of God will reach their final and glorious fulfilment (2 Peter 3:11–13).

FOR FURTHER STUDY

1. Look at some of the great examples of faith in the Old Testament—from Rahab, through Abraham, and Moses holding out his hand over the Red Sea, to Daniel and his friends confronted by a fiery furnace or a den of lions. Are these merely nice stories to tell children? Or do they contain encouragements or challenges for us today?

2. Paul made a comparison between momentary, light afflictions and an eternal weight of glory (2 Cor. 4:17). Which weighs more heavily on your mind and heart? Think about the afflictions that Paul experienced (read, e.g., 2 Cor. 11:23–29). How do you think Paul managed to keep the right balance in his life?

3. One example of Paul's afflictions is the time he spent in jail in Philippi (Acts 16:22–40). How did he respond then and the next day (see vv. 25, 28, 37)?

TO THINK ABOUT AND DISCUSS

1. Have you ever made a clear stand as a Christian, only to wish that you could wind back time and undo what you have just done or said?[3] With the benefit of hindsight, have such moments, when there was no turning back, proved helpful to you as you have moved onwards in your life?

2. How good are you at working with others who have a more adventurous faith than you (e.g. those who might tell you that 'faith is spelled R.I.S.K.', or who are prepared to suggest things that you would rather reflect on before trying them out)? What response should you make if the adventurous 'faith' proves overly optimistic?

3. The 'proof of the pudding' for Ezra would be the end of the journey. Do you feel that Christians think enough about the end of our journey? Are we a people, for example, who would find it hard to sing the old spiritual: 'This world is not my home, I'm just a-passin' through'?

4. What gives us assurance that the overwhelming number of blessings that flow from being a Christian will be experienced by us after our journey here on earth?

Notes

1 At these times we will need to remember above everything else that Christ has done this, and we will need to fix our gaze on him and on the empty tomb.

2 Cited at www.goodreads.com/quotes/show/26859.

3 For those who come from churches that practise believers' baptism, it may have been the moment when you were waiting to be asked questions or to talk about your faith in Christ (I remember how glad I was of a solid pew to hold on to at that moment).

7 Ezra's one-track mind

(Ezra 9:1–10:44)

A CURIOUS THING

"Curiouser and curiouser!' cried Alice (she was so much surprised, that for the moment she quite forgot how to speak good English).' Alice's response came because she was, to use her own words, 'opening out like the largest telescope that ever was'.[1] The book of Ezra has a similar quality in its last two chapters—although whether you would describe it as telescopic or microscopic is open to debate. There is a theme which fills a larger and larger portion of the book, and that theme has a single focus.

LOVE AND MARRIAGE

According to the old musical-hall song, love and marriage 'go together like a horse and carriage'. But as Ezra surveyed the marital arrangements made by those who had returned from exile to the land of God's promise, he saw *disobedience and marriage*, and this appalled him (9:3).

Ezra was, above everything else, a man of God's Word. He had worked hard to get to know it, he used all his skills and abilities to try to understand it and his passion was to follow what God said in it—for the sake of his own life and of the lives of the people he served. He therefore knew the commands God had given to his people about marriage—in particular, about marriage with those who served other gods. In Deuteronomy, for example, in a passage that starts with a list of peoples that is almost identical to the list in Ezra 9:1, God very clearly instructed his people through Moses, 'Do not intermarry with them. Do not give your daughters to their sons or take their daughters for your sons' (Deut. 7:3).

Equally, Ezra understood why God had issued that command and the consequences foretold by God of such disobedience: 'for they will turn your sons away from following me to serve other gods' (Deut. 7:4); 'then you may be sure that the LORD your God will no longer drive out these nations before you. Instead, they will become snares and traps for you ... until you perish from this good land, which the LORD your God has given you' (Josh. 23:13). If Ezra had needed an example of precisely how God's understanding of human nature was realized, he had only to consider the life of one Israel's most favoured and yet most flawed kings—Solomon, the son of David. The sorry summary is found in 1 Kings 11:1–8, with the key in verse 4: 'As Solomon grew old, his wives turned his heart after other gods, and his heart was not fully devoted to the LORD his God, as the heart of David his father had been.'

As Ezra looked at the people around him, one thing was clear. Although these people had only just been given the divine privilege of returning from exile to the land of God's promise, and although they had shown that they would heed God's message in some areas of their lives (see Chapter 4), when it came to this particular area—marriage—they were deaf to God's Word and blind to the consequences that would follow their disobedience.

REACTION

Some years ago, there was a comedy show on UK TV whose leading character responded to every disaster or setback in the same way: 'Oh dear! How sad! Never mind.' Ezra's reaction to the disobedience of the people around him was of a totally different order: 'When I heard this, I tore my tunic and cloak, pulled hair from my head and beard and sat down appalled' (9:3).

There are two initial things to note about this reaction.

Firstly, Ezra was not alone in recognizing the enormity of the rebellion among God's people: he was joined by 'everyone who trembled at the words of the God of Israel' (v. 4).

Secondly, the pulling of his own hair was in direct contrast to Nehemiah's response when confronted with the same folly among God's people (Neh. 13:25—a pastoral response which, I suspect, is not taught in many Bible colleges!). His prayer (Ezra 9:6–15) is nevertheless an identification with the people of God which shares many similarities with the prayers of both Nehemiah (Neh. 1:4–7) and Daniel (Dan. 9:4–6), which are prayed on the basis of what 'we', not 'they', have done.

This begs the following personal questions:

- Does that phrase 'trembled at the words of ... God' (v. 4) have a resonance in my own heart? In other words, would I have been found with those sitting alongside Ezra, sharing in his reaction to the sin of the people and trembling because of what God had to say about their position as rebels before him? Or is it my tendency to gloss over the catastrophic consequences of life choices made by men and women who reject the rule of God's Law?

- Do I find something amusing or even satisfying in the thought of Nehemiah pulling other people's hair (Neh. 13:25), but nothing appealing in the thought of Ezra pulling out hair from his own head? The media constantly reveal to their audiences the errors and fallibilities of others, whether in abusing positions of power and trust, in families as well as in politics, or as seen in the declining standards of society (binge-drinking, vice scandals, financial improprieties and so on). Do I see these as being merely things that 'they' are doing, as I look out from within the confines of the church? Do I then forget that I am part of that society, living within that culture, and commanded by God to be salt and light—and that it is 'we' not 'they' who stand as a nation disgraced by sin (Prov. 14:34; compare Ezra 9:6)?[2]

PAUSE

Before going any further, it is important to try to see why Ezra's reaction was so powerful. The clearest clue is found at the end of 9:2, where we see that Ezra described the people's sins as 'unfaithfulness' (compare v. 4 and 10:6), and that it was the leaders of God's people, those whom God had appointed to draw his people back to a right relationship with him, who had led them in the opposite direction.

Throughout the Old Testament period God demonstrated and repeatedly revealed to his people that he is a God of faithfulness. For example, he revealed himself to Moses as 'The LORD, the LORD, the compassionate and gracious God, slow to anger, abounding in love and faithfulness' (Exod. 34:6). Yet during the same period the people of God had proved themselves to be exactly the opposite; over and over again they had been unfaithful—forgetting and rejecting their relationship with God (see Jer. 3, for example).

The opening chapter of Hosea was a graphic reminder, in the last days of the kingdom of Judah, of the people's unfaithfulness (Hosea 1:2), and the Chronicler summarized the cause of exile to Babylon in these words: 'The people of Judah were taken captive to Babylon because of their unfaithfulness' (1 Chr. 9:1).

Yet no sooner had the exile come to an end and the cloud of God's judgement been lifted than they once again proved that their hearts had not changed; despite the seventy-year lesson of exile they were still only too readily mired in unfaithfulness.

How could this be? Surely those seventy years in exile had given them sufficient time to learn the foolishness of unfaithfulness? What would it take for them truly to change?

RESPONSE

Ezra did not merely react emotionally to what he had heard; he also made a practical response.

His *first* response, which truly revealed his heart, was prayer. But as we look at what is recorded of the time he spent before God (9:5–15), we might think that 'prayer' is too weak a word for the way in which he bared his heart and soul to God, pouring out his awareness of sin, and placing that sin in the context of God's dealings with his people and the people's failings in the past. He acknowledged that God, who is just, had every reason to judge his people and commit them to total destruction (see also, e.g., the second half of 10:14).

Then, at the beginning of verse 15, Ezra fixed his gaze on one specific quality in God's character: his righteousness. In this Ezra found a glimmer of hope, because it was that righteousness that permitted the remnant of God's people to return to the land of promise (just as God had promised through Isaiah and Jeremiah).

But Ezra did not have the confidence to ask anything of God. He simply placed the plight of God's people alongside his assurance of God's righteousness, and left it there.[3]

From his prayer came his *second* response: leading the people in making a covenant. Those who had been prepared by God for this moment gathered around Ezra to encourage and support him, and to show their shared passion for an obedient response to God's Word (10:1–2). That response took the concrete form of a covenant—an agreement entered into by the people through their leaders (v. 5). It is interesting to ponder whether it was the same group of leaders who had actually led the people away from God's path in the first place (9:2) who were now to act as pioneers in bringing the people back to where they should be.

The changes brought about by that covenant were:
- Urgent (10:9)
- Thorough (vv. 12–14—and see the time taken, vv. 16–17)
- Worked through in practical ways (vv. 9, 13)
- Carried through in the face of opposition (v. 15)
- Detailed (vv. 16–44)
- Applied to all within the people of God (vv. 9, 12, 14)

And all this because Ezra himself and the people around him were, or became, those who 'trembled at the words of … God' (9:4).

AVOID THE SQUEEZE

In 1958 a London clergyman, J. B. Phillips, published what he called *The New Testament in Modern English*, a paraphrase aimed at the young people in his parish. He had begun it, starting with the Epistle to the Colossians, in the periods he spent in the bomb shelters during the London Blitz. While this translation is not used much these days, one very memorable phrase—a paraphrase of Romans 12:2—is as relevant today as it was when he coined it: 'Don't let the world around you squeeze you into its own mould.'[4]

Ezra's world—the world that he found when he arrived in Jerusalem—was a world of disobedience and compromise, a world that had, once again, rejected the commands of God for what appeared to be a better and more enticing dance with the followers of other so-called gods. Ezra's response was unequivocal: he would not be squeezed into that mould; and in standing firm in what he knew to be right, others stood with him and together sought and, as we will see later, found the place of God's blessing.

When Paul wrote the book of Romans to a body of God's people living in first-century Rome, the world had two main faces, both of which could exert a squeezing pressure on the lives of his readers—and indeed on Paul himself.

There was the Jewish world from which Paul himself had come ('my own race'—Rom. 9:3). That world could rely on the privileges that they had received from God's hand and see them as a means of gaining favour with and acceptance by God. But Paul knew that the road of reliance on such privileges was quite literally a dead end.

There was also the Roman world—a world which Paul

knew because of the citizenship that he enjoyed (Acts 16:37; 22:25). This was a world that worshipped many gods but had no knowledge of the one true God. By rejecting the truly divine this world debased its followers, and it would one day be exposed in all its horror before God's throne in heaven (Rom. 2:1–16).

It was this dual-faceted world that Paul warned his readers to shun. But what about today? I grew up hearing that it was teenagers who had to face the challenges of 'peer pressure' (i.e. of the people within their world trying to squeeze them into their mould). But actually all of us—whatever our ages, whatever our cultural backgrounds—have pressures on us to conform, to be squeezed into the mould of the world in which we live. Those pressures might come in the form of temptations to find solace in material things, to join a group of friends who head off with the intention of drinking the night away, to access unhealthy websites, to take things that properly belong to our employers, and so on. How do we react to such pressures when they come our way?

One of the greatest dangers is not being able to recognize that the pressures upon us are pressures to conform to an ungodly way of living. I can remember, for example, the pressure towards 'moderation'. It came from the days when the British 'stiff upper lip' was part of the life of Christians and non-Christians alike and when (as in the days of the Wesleys and George Whitefield) to be called an 'enthusiast' was a term of abuse. Still today, terms that imply passion or strong emotion when it comes to matters of faith and belief are often allied with terrorist and dangerously extreme positions. So to have the sort of response that trembles before God, and that places God and love for God above everything else in our lives, is still viewed with suspicion by many around us.

More positively, Paul encouraged his readers to also be transformed by the renewing of their minds (Rom. 12:2). Ezra's mind was certainly transformed—by his knowledge of God and his passion to know God's will lived out in his life and in the lives of those he served. That same passion transformed Paul's life from the day his eyes were opened on the road to Damascus.

Does it rule your life too?

FOR FURTHER STUDY

1. In Isaiah 1, how did the prophet challenge the choices being made by God's people? What solutions—both on their part and on God's— did he suggest?

2. After his commissioning in Isaiah 6, he was given a fairly bleak assessment of the response there would be to his ministry. How did Isaiah react to this assessment? (Do not look for a simple answer; it is seen in the remainder of the book that bears his name.)

3. At the end of Romans 10 Paul thinks back to God's dealings with Isaiah. What encouragements are there for us (perhaps especially v. 20)?

TO THINK ABOUT AND DISCUSS

1. When a preacher preaches God's Word, what emotional response is to be desired among his hearers? If people found it difficult to leave the meeting because they were trembling, would that be a good or bad thing?

2. What priorities ruled the hearts, lives and ambitions of men like Ezra and Paul? How do we translate those priorities into our lives today?

3. Do you find Ezra's 'obsession' (if that is not too strong a word) with the marriage relationships of God's people understandable or utterly bizarre? When did you last hear anyone speak on 2 Corinthians 6:14 and apply it in terms of personal or business relationships, for example?

4. What pressures or situations try to 'squeeze' our lives into a mould today? Are these things always bad, or might some of them be helpful to our Christian lives?

Notes

1 **Lewis Carroll,** *Alice's Adventures in Wonderland* (Harmondsworth: Puffin, 1963), p. 33.

2 Perhaps more significantly: dare I be anything other than honest with myself in acknowledging the reality of my own sin? My sin may never make the papers, but it is never hidden from God's eyes, even down to the deepest depths of the secret places in my heart; and it will one day be revealed (Rom. 2:16).

3 Two of the great Songs of Ascent (Ps. 130; 131) similarly call God's people simply to put their hope in the Lord: to look to him and wait on his sovereign response. There, too, there are no specific requests made of God.

4 Accessed at www.ccel.org/bible/phillips/CP06Romans2.htm.

8 The end of the beginning

(Neh. 8:1–12)

BEGINNING OF THE END

Winston Churchill is famously quoted as saying, 'Now, this is not the end. It is not even the beginning of the end. But it is, perhaps, the end of the beginning.'[1] In our last chapter we reached the end of the book of Ezra. That, however, was not the end of Ezra.

There was a thirteen-year gap between Ezra reaching Jerusalem (Ezra 7:8) and Nehemiah's departure for Jerusalem (Neh. 2:1). What can we deduce about that period?

- Ezra did not change—not in his character, his passions or his priorities. In Nehemiah 8:1 he is called 'Ezra the scribe', which, in the positive sense in which this name is used in the chapter, is a good summary of the qualities revealed, for example, in Ezra 7:6, 10.

- Despite all that Ezra had said and taught, and the changes that had taken place through his ministry (and that of Haggai before him), things were not as they should have been in Jerusalem.

So in Nehemiah 1 we read that Nehemiah, who held a position of privilege in the Persian capital, Susa, heard from his brother, Hanani, 'Those who survived the exile and are back in the province are in great trouble and disgrace. The wall of Jerusalem is broken down, and its gates have been burned with fire' (v. 3).

It would take another book to deal with how God moved Nehemiah to leave Susa and walk round the broken-down walls of Jerusalem. However, one thing that is evident as we read through the book of Nehemiah is that Nehemiah was vitally aware that rebuilt walls and defences relying on arms and armour would not be enough for the people of God. What mattered above everything else was the rebuilding of human hearts through a rebuilding of a right relationship with God!

It was not only Nehemiah who recognized this; it was also the people, who in Nehemiah 8 assembled together and actually *told* Ezra to bring out the Book of the Law of Moses (v. 1)!

Many years ago, a friend of mine, who was at that time pastor of a Baptist church in Sussex, playfully tried to encourage one of his young daughters to call out when he was preaching, 'Give us another hour, Daddy!' I'm not sure that she ever did—nor am I sure how the members of the congregation would have reacted had she done so. But the people in Jerusalem clearly needed no such prompting.

MAN OF THE MOMENT

The slogan from the 1984 film *Ghost Busters* has recently been used in a UK advertising campaign: 'Who you gonna call?' Back in Jerusalem, with the people's longing to go beyond material security and get back to a right relationship with God, and with their certainty that God and his will could be known in 'the Book … of Moses, which the LORD had commanded for Israel' (v. 1), there was only one person whom they could call: Ezra the scribe.

That's quite an interesting question for many churches

today: Who are we going to call? We may recognize that things are not as they should be. That can be true in a large and thriving church, where fulfilling the roles of teaching in Sunday school, playing the organ or in the music group, stewarding and counting the offering does not rest on the shoulders of just two or three members. But it can also be true in a small, mutually encouraging and close-knit church, where everyone knows and, God willing, demonstrates real love for one another. If there is a recognition that things need to be better, who are you most likely to call? Would a 'scribe' be high on anyone's list?

PREPARED PEOPLE

Before looking at what Ezra did, let's turn back to a theme from an earlier chapter: the certainty that God had prepared the people (as well as preparing Ezra) for this day.

There are three key evidences of that preparation:

- It was the people, gathered together 'as one man', that is, utterly united (Neh. 8:1), who told (not asked or suggested) Ezra to bring the Book of Law.
- They had made practical arrangements to enable all the people to hear (v. 4).
- They came with attentive ears (v. 3). They were not, for example, like the disciples in the Garden of Gethsemane, whose eyes 'were heavy' (Matt. 26:43), or the (in)famous young man who fell asleep and then fell out of the window while the apostle Paul preached (Acts 20:9).

Would the events that followed have taken place without this preparation? We don't know, because they were prepared and attentive, and God worked in their hearts.

A SCRIBE AMONG SCRIBES

So Ezra stood up on the platform to read from the Book of the Law, but he was not alone. A number of others stood with him (v. 4).

These were people who had moved from being beneficiaries of Ezra's teaching to being participants in the plans and purposes of God alongside Ezra; they were no longer spectators, but were fully engaged in something that mattered to them as much as it did to Ezra himself. They shared the deep conviction that it was God, through his Word, who could make a real difference to the lives of God's people, and they were willing to work together towards a common goal.

Ezra started the reading. It might seem that for six hours Ezra was alone in what he was doing (v. 3). However, verses 7 and 8 show that he was not alone in the task of unwrapping the wonderful gift of God's Word for God's people: it was his co-workers who gave clarification and explained the meaning (vv. 7–8).

RESPONSIVE PEOPLE

In the next few verses it is clear that the people responded, whether Ezra was speaking to the whole crowd or to just a small part of the crowd. And they also responded to Nehemiah and the Levites: in verse 9 we read that Nehemiah, Ezra and the Levites spoke to them together. Later in that verse we are told that the people had been weeping; it didn't matter whom they had been listening to: they responded in the same way.

The one thing that was common, wherever in the crowd people were standing and whichever teacher was instructing them, was that the Word of God was being read, heard, taught and understood—and responded to.

And what a response it was! It seems to have surprised the leaders so that they had to tell the people to stop weeping and respond in a way more appropriate for a sacred day (vv. 9–10). This was to be a day when the 'joy of the LORD' was their strength.

WHAT'S IN A NAME?

Much of Western culture majors on celebrity. This is not confined to Europe and America: I remember, during a question time at a Bible college in South-East Asia, being asked for my views of the qualities and character of Queen Elizabeth II!

That culture of celebrity has had an impact on the church, which can lead to Christians being more interested in the name of a speaker or preacher than in the message that the person is going to bring. Many may be willing to travel miles to listen to a well-known speaker but will not rouse themselves if the name of the messenger of God's Word is unknown. When God's Word is being preached, is our interest in what God has to say—or in any other, lesser things surrounding the preaching?

And when God's Word is preached, what response should we look for in our own hearts and, if we are preachers, in the hearts of those to whom we are called to minister? If God's Word is 'Sharper than any double-edged sword' and able to 'judge the thoughts and attitudes of the heart [and more]' (Heb. 4:12), should we not long for powerful and potentially painful responses to that Word?

Can we answer anything other than 'Yes'?

WHAT THE WORLD NEEDS NOW

It was Hal David who, together with Burt Bacharach, told us in the 1960s that 'What the world needs now is love'. And, over the years since then, many recording artists have been rewarded for spreading that same message in cover and remixed versions of the song. Some Christians gave a different answer to the greatest need of the world:

If our greatest need had been information,
> God would have sent us an educator.

If our greatest need had been technology,
> God would have sent us a scientist.

If our greatest need had been money,
> God would have sent us an economist.

If our greatest need had been pleasure,
> God would have sent us an entertainer.

But our greatest need was forgiveness,
> so God sent us a Saviour.[2]

That need—and that remedy for the need—remains as true today as it was when God's Son, our Saviour, walked the roads of the Holy Land and, in particular, the road from Jerusalem to Golgotha.

And it is true for all people of all races, cultures, backgrounds and abilities. As Jesus told his disciples just before his death, 'No one comes to the Father except through me' (John 14:6). As Paul reminded the church in Rome, God's gift is 'eternal life in Christ Jesus our Lord' (Rom. 6:23).

But using Ezra as our starting point, can we say specifically what it is that the church needs now, in the early years of the

21st century? Can we assume that lessons from the book of Ezra are lessons that we need to learn today, whatever the size of our churches and in whichever part of the world those churches are to be found? If so, what are those lessons and how can we learn them?

In the early chapters of this book we noted that the book of Ezra is, in some ways, a bit of an oddity. Although the book bears his name, he does not appear until chapter 7 (of ten). More time is spent describing the work of other people (e.g. the altar and temple rebuilding in ch. 3) than is spent on that of Ezra himself. And when it comes to the key event in Ezra's life, which is recorded in the book of Nehemiah, not Ezra, this event occurs only because others (all the people) call on Ezra to bring out God's Book.

While there are no direct parallels in the New Testament, there are similar reminders that the work of God is through the people of God; it is not simply the work of a small group of leaders:

- God's *people* are to be prepared for works of service (Eph. 4).
- Christ died to purchase for himself a *people* eager to do what is good (Titus 2:14).
- It is the *people* of God who are to declare the praises of God who saved us (1 Peter 2:9).
- Paul encouraged his protégé, Timothy, to use God's Word in his ministry because it is that Word that thoroughly equips *people* for every good work (2 Tim. 3:17).

It is not simply that God's people are to be eager to do what is good—although they most certainly should be. Nor is it that God raises up leaders to work while others encourage, approve and applaud what they are doing. Rather, God's people themselves are to be eagerly active in the doing of good work—for in Christ we are created to do good deeds, the glory of which goes to God (Eph. 2:10; Matt. 5:16).

My experience in church leadership has been mixed. Most churches I have served in have been fairly small. There have been times when I have heard people (or was it my own heart?) saying, 'When we have a pastor/minister/full-time worker ...' In churches which are waiting to appoint a new pastor there can be a temptation to put work into 'maintenance mode' until the new pastor comes.

But the lesson from Ezra is that the people of God came to know the blessing of God because they knew what they needed (to hear from God through his Book), they found those (not just Ezra) who would be able not only to read it, but also to explain it (Neh. 8:8), and they then responded powerfully, passionately, and with a clear sense of purpose.

May God grant that our churches are increasingly populated by those who long to hear God speak through his Word and who seek out those who can make God's Word clear. May we then see a heartfelt and powerful response which brings real change to the lands in which we live.

FOR FURTHER STUDY

1. It is said that the book of Deuteronomy is, at its heart, the record of three sermons given by Moses and reflecting on God's dealings with his people over the previous forty years. What challenges did Moses lay before the people at the end of those messages (see, e.g., Deut. 30:11–19)? How is that same stark

choice presented at the end of Jesus's interview with Nicodemus in
John 3:1–21?

2. How should a clear understanding of God's eternal purposes shape
the way we live? (It might help to use 2 Peter 3 as a starting point in
considering this.)

TO THINK ABOUT AND DISCUSS

1. Reflect on the problems that are being faced by your local church,
by a Christian organization that you are involved with, by your local
community or by your family. What sort of person do you think
would be best suited to resolve those issues? Where would a person
with scribe-like qualities come on your list of choices?

2. In today's world, how important is it for those whom God has
appointed as leaders among his people to be good team members?

3. What do you, as a part of a local body of God's people, need
above everything else?

4. How can we ensure that God's people share and continue to
maintain a great longing for the explanation and application of God's
Word to their hearts and lives?

Notes

1 A recording of that famous comment from November 1942 is available on
YouTube: see 'Winston Churchill Speech "The End of the Beginning" 20th
November 1942 (Full Speech)', uploaded 3 September 2009, at
www.youtube.com.

2 **Charles Sell,** Unfinished Business: Helping Adult Children Resolve Their Past
(Portland, OR: Multnomah, 1989), p. 12; quoted at bible.org/illustration/our-
greatest-need.

9 An ongoing event

(Neh. 8:13–10:39)

SUDDEN FLASH OR LONG BURN?

In the UK, early November evenings bring back to me fond childhood memories of a feast for the eyes and also for the stomach. The feast for the eyes came from a starry sky lit up with a glorious fireworks display (feeble in comparison with the amazing professional displays that, for example, ushered in the year 2000—but still spectacular in my childhood memories). The feast for the stomach came in the form of hot dogs (sausages in a roll) and baked potatoes—especially if coated with a dusting of ash from the bonfire in which the baking had taken place. For while fireworks did form an important part of those November evenings, it was actually the bonfire that was central on Bonfire Night (5 November); without a bonfire, the evening, certainly in my childhood days, would have lost its meaning and purpose.[1]

There are two key differences between fireworks and a bonfire. While fireworks are visually stunning, they last only a short time, and their effect is equally transient. However, a properly built bonfire will last a much longer time—indeed, it can last through the night and into the following day. It is only the bonfire that can provide the sustained heat to cook potatoes and through them feed those who are there and provide inner warmth against the cold of a dark evening.

A STEADY BURN

Back to Ezra's day, while the initial reaction to the reading of God's Word was spectacular, the second half of Nehemiah 8 and the two following chapters show that this was not a bright but swiftly fading display, a 'flash in the pan' which failed to go any further.

As a result of what had happened on that first day of the seventh month, there were three things the people wanted to do: to know more, to do more, and to be more certain of their position and standing before God.

KNOW MORE

What was it that they wanted to know, and why? One abiding memory I have is hearing my future mother-in-law saying to her children, when asked why something must be done, 'Because I say so, and the other reasons don't count.' For those who listened to Ezra, though, they did not simply take what he and the other Levites had said at face value; they wanted to 'give attention to the words of the Law' themselves (8:13). They would only be satisfied by learning and understanding for themselves.

It was not that they did not trust Ezra or believe that he was being other than a faithful scribe and servant of the Law of God. It was simply that what was before them was too important for them not to satisfy themselves for themselves. The words they read were those which God himself had commanded through Moses (v. 14). As the apostle Peter puts it in 2 Peter 1:21, 'For prophecy never had its origin in the will of man, but men spoke from God as they were carried along by the Holy Spirit.'

There was a real immediacy about their desire to learn from God through his Law. They were studying his Law in the seventh month, and what they learned was what God wanted them to do in the seventh month (v. 14).

How often, when I pick up my Bible to read it, or sit down on a Sunday to hear God's messenger explain it, do I expect (or even desire) God to have something to say to me for that particular day? (It's worth reading Ps. 95:7–8 and its application in Heb. 3–4.)

DO MORE

The people in Ezra's day did not only want to know more; they also longed to do more. They were a people with a willing and obedient heart.

So, when they learnt about the festival and God's instruction for his people to live in booths, their response was not to file this information away for another day but to go out, build booths and live in them (vv. 14–18). They wanted to do what God required of them.

The final phrase from verse 17 is a wonderful encouragement for us. As the people listened to God, determined to do what God asked, and then did indeed do what God commanded them, they were filled with great joy.

Many years ago I was introduced to a way of trying to store parts of God's Word in my memory. One of the key verses used about faith was a reminder of how important it is not only to know what God commands, but also to do what he commands: 'Whoever has my commands *and obeys them*, he is the one who loves me' (John 14:21, emphasis added).

Nehemiah 8 finishes with a clear indication that the people

did exactly what God had commanded for all the days of the festival. They continued obeying him throughout the festival to the very end. They kept an eye on what was required of them on each day, acting 'in accordance with the regulation' (v. 18). This was God's will, and they could think of nothing better than walking in that will and obeying God's Law.

BE MORE CERTAIN

This attitude wasn't just for the days of the festival. Chapter 9 leads us through a series of events which were designed to secure this newly rediscovered relationship with God.

Once again it starts with reading from the Book of the Law (v. 3). That led to a time when the people of God worshipped the God whom they served. Part of that time of worship involved the people confessing their sins openly to God (v. 3).

Verses 5–37 form a sandwich of praise. Up to verse 15 the focus is on God ('you'). From verse 32 (perhaps even from v. 29) the focus of attention returns to God—his person, character and actions. In between, in verses 16 to 28, there is a different focus of attention introduced in verse 16 by 'but'. That 'but' directs us to look at the failings, the disobedience, the rebellion and ultimately the stupidity of the people of God.

Verses 36 and 37 acknowledge the consequences of this stupidity. And verse 38 speaks of a new agreement, a new covenant, something that would change the course of history—in the words of Jeremiah, to give God's people 'hope and a future' (Jer. 29:11).

Such a covenant is only as good as the party on the other side. This covenant, however, flowed from a remembering of God as the one who 'keeps his covenant of love' (v. 32). It was on the basis of that certain and secure knowledge that the people entered into a new agreement with God.

NEW COVENANT

According to the old children's chorus, 'Read your Bible, pray every day and you'll grow, grow, grow.' Conversely, if you neglect to read and pray, you will 'shrink, shrink, shrink'.[2] Which of these two changes in the size, quality, depth and passion of your Christian life has occurred in the last month, year or even decade?

Is your life as a child of God growing or diminishing? You may no longer have the invincibility of youth (it used to be said that employers should employ teenagers while they still know everything!). There may be increased responsibilities that have come with house ownership, marriage, children or even grand- and great-grandchildren. There may even be financial, health or memory problems challenging the choices we need to make regarding where we live, the occupations we could pursue or activities we could enjoy. But do these changes and problems have a negative effect on your relationship with God and your walk with him?

When the Bible speaks about our Christian lives it is clear that we should expect and desire growth and development. We are to:

- long for God's precious feeding through his Word so that we might 'grow up in [our] salvation' (1 Peter 2:2)
- grow up in all things into Christ (Eph. 4:15)
- be built up and built together as God's people (Eph. 4:12; 1 Peter 2:5)
- continue to live in Christ (Col. 2:6); someone who loses

connection with Christ can no longer grow as he or she should (Col. 2:19)

The Bible understands the weaknesses of our human nature and recognizes that the growth path will not always be easy or lacking in ups and downs (Jesus describes it as a narrow way, Matt. 7:14). However, the clear goal is for growth that will increasingly fit us to stand around God's throne in glory when our life of service here on earth reaches its conclusion.

For the people of Ezra's day, they did not merely see growth as a necessary or natural extension of their new covenant relationship with God; they wanted it, longed for it and desired it with an intensity that was reflected in the manner of their response to what they heard from Ezra and his fellow scribes.

I remember some years ago being in a church prayer meeting and hearing a person pleading with God to send people to serve him in a particular part of the world. I don't remember which part of the world, nor why the need was so great at that time. What I do remember, however, was that the person prayed that God would send 'young people' to do that work, and that the person praying was no longer in the first flush of youth. At that time I was a fair bit younger than I am today, and it may be for that reason that I remember the prayer because it seemed unfair. Why should the person praying try to exclude one of God's possible answers to prayer: 'Do it yourself'?[3] Yet, over the intervening years, I have found it harder to be involved in the 'doing'—the outworking of a proper response to God in appreciation of all that God has done for me.

As a student and during the years that followed I had the privilege of being involved in summer missions and camps and also outreach activities with students who had come to study English in the UK; more recently I have 'needed' to guard my holidays and so find it very hard to consider taking time off for, say, a Holiday Bible Club week. When I was younger I would think little of coming home from a day's work (involving, for some years, commuting from London) to go out to evening meetings or activities two or three times a week. Now—and I don't need to be particularly honest with myself to acknowledge it—I struggle to do much at all when I come in after a day at the computer; the idea of going out again is hard to contemplate.

One of the few new opportunities to serve God that have been added to my life in recent years came simply because my brain and mouth could not form the word 'No' quickly enough. But that opportunity, as it has developed, has been a reminder both of the privilege it is to be able to serve our Saviour King in the work of his kingdom and also of the blessings that flow to us, when we do serve him, and, hopefully, also to those he calls us to serve.

In my church's songbook one song starts by asking the question, 'What's your treasure? What's your favourite thing?' It gives the answer that 'it's better if your treasure's in heaven …'[4] I wonder how much you would mean it if you sang that song today.

FOR FURTHER STUDY

1. At the end of his life, Joshua told the people to make a choice about whether or not to enter into a renewed covenant with God. How clear was the response the people made (Josh. 24:21)? How long did that response hold good (Judg. 2:7, 10–11)? What had changed?

2. In the parables of the lost sheep, coin and son (Luke 15) what brings rejoicing in heaven? What joy does it bring on earth (i.e. to us) when we see God at work in someone's life?

3. What do those parables and some of the linked events leading up to the meeting with Zacchaeus in Luke 19 tell us about God's plans and purposes in Jesus (see, e.g., Luke 19:10)?

TO THINK ABOUT AND DISCUSS

1. What do you anticipate will happen when you read God's Word, or when someone reads God's Word to you or seeks to explain God's Word by faithful preaching?

2. What do you want to do with what you have read, heard or understood from God's Word? How often do you expect to have to put what you learn into practice between one Sunday morning and the next?

3. In what ways has your relationship with God changed since you first came to know about him or first responded to him as your Saviour and King? Have there been times when William Cowper's line would ring more bells than you would like to acknowledge: 'Where is the blessedness I knew when first I saw the Lord?'[5]

4. Ezra and the people of God in Jerusalem made a covenant together to obey God. Might you find it helpful to agree with other *people to do something together for God—whether it be to meet together to pray, to engage in an activity such as visiting nearby care homes, to involve yourself with a social-action project in your area or to work together to lead a service in your own or a nearby church?*

Notes

1   You can find out the meaning of Bonfire Night in **Clive Anderson's** *Gunpowder, Treason and Plot* (Leominster: Day One, 2005).
2   www.churchbusnews.com/downloads/ReadYourBiblePrayEveryDay.txt.
3   I have heard people speak of God's five answers to prayer: Yes; No; Wait; Do it yourself; and Mind your own business (or, as **C. S. Lewis** puts it in *The Horse and His Boy*, 'That is someone else's story' (London: Geoffrey Bles/Bodley Head, 1963)).
4   **Phil and Ruth West,** 2007.
5   **William Cowper,** 'Oh, For a Closer Walk with God', 1772.

10 A three-tone chord

(Neh. 10:30–39)

LISTS

Is yours a family that relies on lists? My wife is a great believer in them. She is a teacher, and every school holiday almost the first thing that happens is that a list is prepared. On it will be all the key things that need to happen before school starts again. These will include things that are necessary for the start of the new school term, plans for any changes to the house or garden, items to buy and potentially much, much more.

For her, a list is a means to mark achievement. Every item that is crossed off the list is a mark of success: a job completed, a task fulfilled. Indeed, just the other day there was a sound of glee when she suddenly realized that she had achieved something on her list—even though she had forgotten it was on the list.

For one of our friends, however, lists have a totally different meaning. He sees them as a mark of failure. Every time he looks at the list his wife has prepared, he just sees items that are still outstanding. While he was still working, he would have times away from his desk which we knew as 'Honeydew' weeks but for him actually meant 'Honey, do ...'—a period in which he would be given a set of tasks to do at home. As the week went by, it was the incomplete tasks that loomed larger and larger in his mind.

COVENANT LIST

When it came to the people re-establishing their covenant relationship with God, they did so with a list (vv. 30–39).

This list had both success and failure criteria built into it. It contained promises and obligations which they undertook to perform. If those undertakings were met, it meant success. If those undertakings were not met, it meant failure.

Two key elements to this list determined how possible it would be for success to be achieved and failure avoided. The first related to the difficulty of the individual promises; the second, to the number of items on the list. The greater the number, the greater the danger of distraction, lack of focus, or people simply forgetting what it was they were supposed to do.

In the legends of ancient Greece, Heracles (Hercules) had twelve tasks or labours. In England, the stories of Arthur and the Knights of the Round Table are full of quests to be pursued and tasks to be performed—all of which were designed as tests to prove whether or not the individual was a worthy knight. And in history itself, God gave to his people, through his servant Moses, ten headline commands.

SIGN OF THREE

However, Nehemiah and the other leaders of the people did not simply go back to those ten commandments. What we find in 10:30–39 are only three key commitments—but those three were to be at the heart of their relationship with God. The people had been rescued by God, brought back by God's power and mercy to live in and around Jerusalem, and they now wanted to reforge a lasting and living relationship with God. These three commitments were:

- Not to marry their sons and daughters to the people from neighbouring lands—a promise that God would come first in the people's affections. This should come as no surprise given that Ezra was a prime mover among the teachers of God's Word, for this promise dealt with the exact same concern that had consumed Ezra in his teaching, praying and instruction in the last section of his book.
- To keep God's day holy.
- To 'not neglect the house of our God' (v. 39).

WHY THESE THREE?

But why choose these three specific promises to form the foundations for their new relationship with God?

If we turn back to the Ten Commandments (Exod. 20; Deut. 5), we see a distinction between the first four commands, which have to do with the people's relationship with God, and the last six, which concern the people's relationships with one another. So Paul, in Romans 13, could summarize the last six commands with the second of Jesus's 'great commands': 'love your neighbour as yourself' (Rom. 13:9).

At this point in their history, the people of Nehemiah's day needed and wanted a restored relationship with God. It could be argued that their relationships with one another had already been forged through their shared experiences, hardship and work in the rebuilding of the walls of the city. It was their relationship with God that was their priority now. So those three commitments related specifically to their relationship with God (having nothing to distract them from their relationship with him), with God's holy day and with the work of God in the house of God.

There were those among the returning exiles who remembered the house of God as it had been before the exile (Ezra 3:12). When Solomon had originally dedicated the temple, he had spelled out to the people of God that God's house was supremely significant to God's people in many ways (2 Chr. 6:14–42), the foundational one being because the temple was the place where God's Name would be known (2 Chr. 6:8–10).

WHAT'S IN A NAME?

In the UK, children are given all kinds of names these days; sometimes it seems that 'the stranger, the better' is the order of the day. But names are important. As a lawyer I prepare wills, and I need to make sure I have the full and correct names not only of the person who is making the will, but also of those who are to receive benefit from it.

When our children were about to be born, we discovered books which not only gave lists of possible children's names, but also gave their meanings (there was no Internet to find the information in those days). And for us, at least, meaning mattered as much as anything else when we chose our children's names. In the Bible, though, when a name is mentioned, it is often that name's meaning that really matters. For example, the names of Isaiah's two sons sum up the whole of his message—both the destruction that would come and the hope that would follow (Isa. 7:3; 8:1–4), Abram's name ('exalted father') was changed to Abraham ('father of many') following the birth of his son; Ruth's mother-in-law Naomi asked people to call her by another name, Mara ('bitter'), because of her bitterness—and many more examples could be given.

When it comes to God, the name chosen for the Son of God when he entered the world as the child of Mary was overflowing with meaning. When God first met with Moses, God said that it was by his Name that he was to be known (Exod. 3:14–15). God's Name more than reflects his character—it is an expression and overflowing of who he is.

So, by offering support to the house of God, the place where God's Name was to be known, Nehemiah, Ezra and all those who joined them in entering this covenant relationship with God were once again expressing their determination to put God—the real, living, eternal and all-powerful Creator, Redeemer and King—first above all that they did and all their desires.

BARE NECESSITIES

In Walt Disney's version of Kipling's *Jungle Book*, Baloo sings to Mowgli and tells him to look for the bare necessities of life. This means stripping away Mowgli's worries and strife. The people in Ezra and Nehemiah's day also made promises to focus on the bare essentials of their new covenant relationship with God. What are the key elements of a true covenant relationship with God?

In the New Testament that same question—or something like it—is asked on a number of occasions.

- The jailer at Philippi asked, 'What must I do to be saved?' (Acts 16:30).
- A rich young man asked, 'What must I do to inherit eternal life?' (Mark 10:17).
- The crowd, having listened to Peter speaking of the crucifixion and resurrection of Jesus Christ, simply asked, 'What shall we do?' (Acts 2:37).

This book is not the place for a detailed examination of the contexts surrounding these and similar questions in the New Testament. However, in these contexts and in the answers given, one key theme emerges: what matters is our response to and relationship with Jesus Christ.

So:

- The jailer was told that he needed to believe in the Lord Jesus.
- The rich young ruler was challenged to think what he really meant when he called Jesus a 'good teacher', and whether he was truly prepared to give up his riches and follow Jesus—even for the sake of eternal life.[1]
- Peter's response was that the people had to 'repent', a word that has the same root as that used by Jesus in Luke 24:47.[2] Repentance is something that starts with a change of mind about 'this Jesus, whom you crucified' (Acts 2:36).

Again and again in the New Testament there are examples which show that the irreducible minimum to a right relationship with God and to receiving God's gift of eternal life—a real and secure hope for the life we live here on earth as well as for the life after death (or after Jesus's return)—is to be found in Christ and in Christ alone.

So, for example, Paul tells us that there is no condemnation for those who are in Christ (Rom. 8:1), that the free gift of God is eternal life in Christ Jesus (Rom. 6:23) and that all God's promises are 'Yes' in Christ Jesus (2 Cor. 1:20).

Many more examples could be given (a search of a computer-based concordance reveals over eighty examples of the simple phrase 'in Christ' used by Paul and other New Testament writers). And these examples—along with the glorious certainties that surround them—were distilled by our Christian forefathers in the days of the Reformation into three truths that stood alone together: that our new relationship with God is by grace *alone*, through faith *alone*, in Christ *alone*. More poetically, the same certainty was found more than 500 years before the Reformation in the words of the well-known hymn '*Rob tu mo bhoile, a Comdi cride*' ('Be Thou My Vision, O Lord of My Heart):

Riches I heed not, nor man's empty praise,
Thou mine Inheritance, now and always:
Thou and Thou only, first in my heart,
High King of heaven, my Treasure Thou art.[3]

A more modern hymn expresses the same truth:

In Christ alone my hope is found …[4]

  Is God your High King, your Treasure? Is your hope found in him alone?

FOR FURTHER STUDY

1. *In what ways were the names given to Isaiah's sons or Hosea's son and daughter, for example, summaries of the messages of their ministries? (See Isa. 7 :3; 8:1–4 and Hosea 1:4, 6; see your translation's marginal notes for the meanings of these names.)*

2. *At the very end of Luke's Gospel, Jesus tells his disciples that two key things have to happen to him (Luke 24:46). What are they, and where in the Old Testament were these prophesied, as Jesus says they were?*

3. *What two-stranded message is then entrusted to the Christian church? (See Luke 24:47.)*

TO THINK ABOUT AND DISCUSS

1. *What dangers are there in reducing the call of God on our lives or in adding too much flesh to the bare bones of God's message as summed up in the two words 'repentance' and 'forgiveness' in Luke 24:47?*

2. *Are there things in your circumstances at the moment which could be coming between you and God, preventing him from taking his proper place in your life?*

3. *In what areas of your life, and in what ways, could you show more clearly and distinctly the love you have for your Saviour King?*

4. *Ask that same question in terms of the activities and priorities of your church or other Christian organizations with which you are involved.*

Notes

1 For an excellent examination of Mark's account of the meeting between Jesus and the rich young ruler, see **Walter J. Chantry,** *Today's Gospel: Authentic or Synthetic?* (Edinburgh: Banner of Truth (n.d.)). The importance of his question is at the heart of the Christianity Explored course (see www.christianityexplored.org).

2 *Metanoia* (from the Greek μετάνοια, changing one's mind). See 'Metanoia (theology)' at www.en.wikipedia.org.

3 Attributed to **Dallan Forgaill,** 8th century; trans. from ancient Irish to English by Mary E. Byrne, 1905, and versed by Eleanor H. Hull, 1912 (www.cyberhymnal.org).

4 **Stuart Townend and Keith Getty,** 2001.

11 The missing piece

(Neh. 13)

I REMEMBER THIS

The story is told of a village vicar who preached one Sunday on Christ's new commandment, 'Love one another', in John 13:34–35. The next week his congregation were slightly surprised to hear him preach the same sermon, word for word, once again—and the same the next week and the week after that. At last, one of the members of the congregation plucked up the courage to ask the vicar why the same sermon was being preached week in, week out. The reply came back: 'Are you doing it yet?'

Repetition can indeed reinforce lessons; in this case, however, the frequency used and failure to include other material might be counted as taking things to an extreme. But there are other reasons why a statement or a request might be repeated. For example, the person making the statement might be uncertain or forgetful, or the people to whom the statement is made might be poor hearers or unwilling to respond.

A NECESSARY PRESENCE

In chapter 13, Nehemiah calls three times to God to 'remember'. The first time is in verse 14: 'Remember me for this, O my God.' He called on God to remember because the support for God's house and the Levites and others involved in the work of God's house had started to fail and needed to be revived (vv. 4–13).

The second time is in verse 22. This time it is because the Lord's day was being abused, and Nehemiah had had to institute simple and practical solutions to ensure that the day was observed within the walls of Jerusalem (vv. 15–22).

The third time is in verse 29 and is because of the return to marriage relationships with the enemies of God and God's work, with those who were clearly and overtly drawing people away from God. The supreme example was one of the sons of Joiada, the son of God's high priest. He had married into the family of Sanballat the Horonite (v. 28; Neh. 2:10, 19; 4:1, 7–8; 6:1–2 give a flavour of just how dreadful that marriage must have been to Nehemiah). What a rejection of God's purposes that was by the one who entered that marriage bond: a man whose grandfather had been the first to start work on the repairs to the wall (3:1).

Three promises, three hurdles, three failures (failures at each of the three points of promise made by the people just a short while before)—except when Nehemiah was around. The failures started and continued when he was away (13:6). It is when he came back that remedies were put in place to get things back to where they should be, to where the covenant promises declared that they would be.

Without Nehemiah: problem. With Nehemiah: solution.

HAVE WE BEEN HERE BEFORE?

This is a reflection of a disease that afflicted the people of God throughout the Old Testament period. While there was a godly leader—be it Moses, Joshua, David, Hezekiah or Josiah—the people were able to maintain (at least in part) a faithful following of God and his ways. When the leader was called away from the people and into God's presence, it was the start of a slippery slope—a downgrade from which only God's intervention with a new leader and a new voice to challenge the conscience of the people would restore them.

This problem was recognized by a number of the leaders in their own lifetimes. For example, Moses and Joshua challenged the people to choose between life and death and whom they would serve (Deut. 30:11–20; Josh. 24:15).

In Nehemiah's day, the additionally heart-breaking aspect of this downward spiral was that the people had recognized it in those who went before, had stated it clearly and unequivocally in the words of the covenant (9:16–31) and yet still, despite everything, did exactly the same. They were no different from their forefathers; indeed, in many ways they were actually much worse, because:

- They knew exactly what would happen if they failed and forgot to obey God.
- There were only three hurdles, and they weren't insurmountable (see Deut. 30:11–13).

Indeed, when Nehemiah was around, it was almost a case of 'Easy—no problem!' But no sooner had the dust from his donkey settled over the horizon than the same age-old problems surfaced and the same disastrous outcome loomed over the opposite horizon.

IS THERE A WAY OUT?

At this point, we do need to remind ourselves that in terms of biblical history, we are at the very end of the Old Testament period.

Although in our Bibles more than half the Old Testament is to be found after the books of Ezra and Nehemiah (and Esther), in chronological terms nothing follows except a void in which the judgement of God fell and the people of God were scattered throughout the empire of Alexander of Macedon and the republic of Rome. We are left at this point in history with a desperate and depressing question: Is there then no hope at all?

The people had failed to learn the lessons of history. They had been served by one of the most passionate leaders of God's people—Ezra (as well as Nehemiah). Ezra's ministry had also been supported by the work and service of Haggai, Zechariah, Jeshua and Zerubbabel—among many others.

Ezra's ministry had been blessed, resulting in a powerful change in the hearts and lives of the people he served, and it had appeared that a new start, a new hope had arrived.

And yet—and yet; three disastrous failures summarize not only the books of Ezra and Nehemiah, but the whole of the Old Testament. Was there any possibility that the promise of God through Jeremiah, to give his people 'hope and a future' (29:11), might ultimately bear fruit? Yes!

For God, this stark reminder of the fallibility and failings of his people would have come as no surprise. He knew their hearts, just as he still knows our hearts today. With the certainty of that knowledge he had been preparing his people—indeed, preparing the whole of his creation—for a solution that would deal irrevocably with the heart of the problem, which is ultimately a problem of the heart.

Over and over again in the Old Testament we see that, while

men and women of true faith in God led the people—acted as bridges between God and his people—there was hope and peace, and the promises of God saw their fulfilment. But when those bridges were broken down—most often by death but at other times by disobedience—disaster followed. The only way to break this cycle of delight turning to despair was to provide a permanent solution, one which would never know defeat through disobedience and would never be separated from the people by death. This sinless and eternal solution could only be found in the person of God himself—the one Paul describes as the only mediator between God and man, 'the man Christ Jesus' (1 Tim. 2:5).

That solution would also involve a change in the fickle hearts of God's people—people who, like Joiada's son, could make a promise one day and break it the next. This would be done by moving the relationship between God and humankind from an outward obedience to a set of external rules (on tablets of stone or books of law) to a new heart on which the desire and determination to follow God and walk in his ways would be written (see Jer. 31:33).

For that to be possible, however, not only was it necessary for a permanent mediator to be found in the person of God the Son, it was also necessary for God the Holy Spirit to make his home in the lives of all who would know the blessings of this true new covenant between God and humankind. Ezekiel 36:26–27 and 37:14 contain two of a number of promises that God made with increasing frequency and clarity as the prophets of the old covenant pointed forward to the new covenant to come: 'And I will put my Spirit in you and move you to follow my decrees and be careful to keep my laws … I will put my Spirit in you and you will live, and I will settle you in your own land. Then you will know that I the LORD have spoken, and I have done it, declares the LORD.' God had promised to take out of us our hearts of stone and put in us hearts of flesh, and to put his Spirit within us (see also Isa. 44:3; Joel 2:29). These passages may well have been in Jesus's mind when he was talking to Nicodemus (John 3:1–21).

Ezra—for all his passion, his faithfulness and his willing obedience to God—could not achieve a lasting relationship between God and his people without the promised indwelling of God the Holy Spirit. None of us can achieve or know a lasting (eternally lasting) relationship with God without the promised indwelling of God the Holy Spirit. Do you know God's indwelling presence in your life?

NO BUSH TO BEAT AROUND

In Galatians 3:2, Paul asked the Christians in Galatia, 'Did you receive the Spirit by observing the law, or by believing what you heard?'

Paul clearly cared passionately about the purity of their theology and the one and only gospel message which had been proclaimed to them and which they appeared to be deserting (1:6–9). He also clearly cared about the lifestyles that they were living as those who professed to be followers of the Lord Jesus Christ (this letter contains one of the clearest descriptions of the character of a child of God who is keeping in step with God's will and purposes for his or her life—5:22–25). Yet his question related to the work of God the Holy Spirit in their lives. For Paul, the thing that marked out the Galatians as Christians was their receiving of the Holy Spirit.

Paul's knowledge of the Old Testament made it clear to him that all God's promises could only be truly known when a person's heart and life were transformed by God the Holy Spirit coming to live within that person. He was quite clear to the Galatians: the coming of the Holy Spirit into a person's life was what marked him or her out as a true new-covenant child of God. Unless someone has had that experiential change, he or she cannot be a true child of God. Or, as Jesus put it to Nicodemus, unless someone is born again 'of the Spirit', he or she cannot enter the kingdom of God (John 3:5–8).

Over the last hundred years there appears to have been a polarization among Christians. Some have emphasized the ongoing work of God the Holy Spirit after a person's conversion, which has resulted in a downplaying of the utter necessity of the Holy Spirit's place in a person's new birth. On the other hand (and I fear I have been among them), others have reacted against this emphasis by downplaying the work and role of God the Holy Spirit altogether.

In church history, however, in the days when the wonders of biblical Christianity were being rediscovered by men like Martin Luther and his contemporaries, the place and work of God the Holy Spirit were considered in great detail. So, for example, John Calvin's *Institutes of the Christian Religion* contains much about the Holy Spirit and his work. Oliver Cromwell's one-time chaplain John Owen published much material dealing with the Holy Spirit.[1]

But Paul's concern when writing to the church in Galatia was to do with their experience, not their academic knowledge. He knew that they knew—and he knew that they knew that he knew—that when the gospel message had been preached and they had trusted in that message through faith, they had received the Holy Spirit, just as God had promised. They had received him as a fulfilment of the promises of God originally made to Abraham. As a result of those promises being fulfilled, they had received the blessing given to Abraham (Gal. 3:14): of redemption and of adoption as children into God's family (3:26, 29; 4:4–7).

One of the lessons I have learned as a lawyer operating under the British legal system is just how all-encompassing the law of adoption is (or, at least, used to be) when it comes to the inheritance rights of an adopted child. A person adopted into a new family ceased to have any rights or interests in the family from which he or she had come. Instead, this person came to have exactly the same rights and interests as any other child in the new family of which he or she had become a part. Likewise, in biblical terms, Paul could say in Romans that as God's adopted children are not only heirs of God's kingdom, we are—even more gloriously—co-heirs with Christ; that is, we have exactly the same inheritance as God's one and only begotten Son (Rom. 8:17). One of the rights, privileges and joys of this inheritance is to be able to call God our 'Father' ('*Abba*, Father'—Rom. 8:15–16; Gal. 4:6).

And all this flows from the actual and experiential receiving of God the Holy Spirit into our lives. With the Holy Spirit, we are children of God, we have new hearts, we are born-again citizens of God's kingdom and heirs of the promise and part of God's family for all eternity.

That receiving of the Holy Spirit comes through faith in Christ: faith in his saving work as revealed in the gospel message (Gal. 3:26). 'For it is by grace you have been saved, through faith—and this not from yourselves, it is the gift of God—not by works, so that no one can boast. For we are God's workmanship, created in Christ Jesus to do good works, which God prepared in advance for us to do' (Eph. 2:8–10).

FOR FURTHER STUDY

1. Follow the development of God's promise of a new-covenant relationship with him through the Old Testament—for example, in the books of Isaiah and Jeremiah. Why was this new covenant necessary?

2. Look at the promises God made in Ezekiel 36. What specific things did God promise that he would do? How would this affect a person's relationship with him?

3. The promise and reality of God the Holy Spirit at work in people's lives goes back to Exodus (31:1–3) and is seen again in the life of David before he became king (1 Sam. 16:13). What is the difference between these examples and the promise for those in a new-covenant relationship with God?

TO THINK ABOUT AND DISCUSS

1. Have you ever let God down? How did you feel, and how did you respond to such failure? (Which is more helpful: pulling out your hair (Ezra 9:3), or a reflection on 1 John 1:8–10?)

2. Who has had a positive influence on how you live for God and the things that matter most in your Christian life? What is it about this person that has been such a positive influence on you?

3. How well do you cope with pressures when you have to face them

alone? How might it be (or how is it) helpful for you to have other Christians around you—in your workplace or in your home?
4. *Taking words from Romans 8:16, how has God the Holy Spirit witnessed to your spirit in recent days about your relationship with God? How has God's presence and working in your life enabled you to keep in step with him (Gal. 5:25)?*

Note

1 In particular, readers are referred to **John Owen,** *The Holy Spirit: The Treasures of John Owen for Today's Readers* (abridged and made easy to read by R. J. K. Law; Edinburgh: Banner of Truth, 1998).

About Day One:

Day One's threefold commitment:

- TO BE FAITHFUL TO THE BIBLE, GOD'S INERRANT, INFALLIBLE WORD;

- TO BE RELEVANT TO OUR MODERN GENERATION;

- TO BE EXCELLENT IN OUR PUBLICATION STANDARDS.

I continue to be thankful for the publications of Day One. They are biblical; they have sound theology; and they are relative to the issues at hand. The material is condensed and manageable while, at the same time, being complete—a challenging balance to find. We are happy in our ministry to make use of these excellent publications.

JOHN MACARTHUR, PASTOR-TEACHER, GRACE COMMUNITY CHURCH, CALIFORNIA

It is a great encouragement to see Day One making such excellent progress. Their publications are always biblical, accessible and attractively produced, with no compromise on quality. Long may their progress continue and increase!

JOHN BLANCHARD, AUTHOR, EVANGELIST AND APOLOGIST

Visit our website for more information and to request a free catalogue of our books.

www.dayone.co.uk
www.dayonebookstore.com

Face2face series

Title	Author	ISBN
Face2face Daniel	Ellsworth, Roger	978–1–84625–223–5
Face2face David Volume 1	Bentley, Michael	978–1–84625–040–8
Face2face David Volume 2	Bentley, Michael	978–1–84625–015–6
Face2face Elijah	Robinson, Simon J	978–1–84625–011–8
Face2face Elisha	Winter, Jim	978–1–84625–113–9
Face2face Ezra	Hughes, Chris	978–1–84625–298–3
Face2face Joseph	Ellsworth, Roger	978–1–84625–293–8
Face2face Judas	Wheeler, Andrew	978–1–84625–192–4
Face2face Paul (Book 1)	Ellsworth, Roger	978–1–84625–294–5
Face2face Paul (Book 2) (Forthcoming)	Ellsworth, Roger	978–1–84625–295–2
Face2face Rahab	Hughes, Chris	978–1–84625–135–1
Face2face Samuel	Ellsworth, Roger	978–1–84625–039–2
Face2face Sennacherib	Anderson, Clive	978–1–84625–076–7
Face2face Simon Peter	Ellsworth, Roger	978–1–84625–092–7
Face2face Tamar, Bathsheba and Tamar	Jones, Julia	978–1–84625–141–2

Face2face Rahab— Encountering the woman snatched from destruction

CHRIS HUGHES

80PP, PAPERBACK

ISBN 978–1–84625–135–1

Can the short account of a brief incident from the life of a woman of dubious character say anything to us today—a woman who lived over 3,000 years ago and whose city was doomed to destruction? Yes indeed!

Here is a very readable devotional book with encouraging insights into a lesser-known but surprisingly significant Bible character—Rahab. Throughout the story of this Jericho call-girl, the amazing grace and purpose of God is seen in both the Old and New Testaments.
—*David Abernethie, previously a pastor in Bristol and East Cheam and on the staff of the Evangelical Alliance*

In less than a dozen short, punchy chapters, we are introduced to the mini-drama of the heroine Rahab in her ruin and redemption, set against the backcloth of 'the greatest story ever told' of the Joshua/Jesus the hero of it all. An excellent resource.
—*Dr Steve Brady, Principal, Moorlands College, England*

Face to face with David volume 1— Encountering the man after God's heart

MICHAEL BENTLEY

96PP, PAPERBACK

ISBN 978–1–84625–040–8

Raised in obscurity, young David would not have featured on a list of candidates for the future king of Israel-but God had different ideas! Read, here, about how God's magnificent plan unfolded in the life of this remarkable man and in the lives of those around him.

Michael Bentley worked as a bookshop manager and served in the British army before his call to the ministry. He has a diverse background, which includes broadcasting, teaching Religious Education, and holding pastorates in Surrey, South East London, and Berkshire, while being closely involved with his local community. Now retired, he lives in Bracknell with his wife, Jenny, and has five children and six grandchildren. He is the author of ten books.

Michael Bentley has an enviable knowledge of the Bible and an admirably simple way of relating its events, and then interweaving the stories with their relevance to our life. Thus, we see how the actions related in the bible can still be appropriate today in the way we live our lives.

FRAN GODFREY, BBC RADIO 2 NEWSREADER/ANNOUNCER

Face to face David volume 2— Encountering the king who reigned in power

MICHAEL BENTLEY

144PP, PAPERBACK

ISBN 978–1–84625–015–6

Raised in obscurity, shooting to prominence in the nation of Israel, David became a powerful figure and everyone loved him—well, not quite everyone. Read about his battles, his triumphs, and also his troubles in this engaging, easy-to-use guide.

Michael Bentley worked as a bookshop manager and served in the British army before his call to the ministry. He has a diverse background, which includes broadcasting, teaching Religious Education, and holding pastorates in Surrey, South East London, and Berkshire, while being closely involved with his local community. Now retired, he lives in Bracknell with his wife, Jenny, and has five children and six grandchildren. He is the author of ten books.

'Michael Bentley treats the life of David in a simple, straightforward fashion, never losing sight throughout of the practical significance he has for us, and constantly holding before us David's greater Son, the Lord Jesus. A very good and satisfying book!'
ROGER ELLSWORTH, PASTOR OF IMMANUEL BAPTIST CHURCH, BENTON, ILLINOIS, USA, AND BIBLE COMMENTATOR

'… a book which is full of wisdom …'
CHRIS PORTER, EASTHAMPSTEAD BAPTIST CHURCH, ENGLAND

Face to face with Elijah— Encountering Elijah the fiery prophet

SIMON J ROBINSON

80PP, PAPERBACK

ISBN 978–1–84625–011–8

Elijah, the fiery prophet, lived in a time of intense spiritual darkness. People were openly disobeying God's commands, and true worship seemed to have been all but snuffed out. And yet God was still at work! Bringing the power of his word and Spirit into this situation, he used Elijah to break the darkness and to draw people back to himself. This fascinating encounter with Elijah draws out his significance in God's plan and provides us with practical help to live for Christ in the spiritual darkness of the twenty-first century. Each chapter includes questions and points for reflection, making this an ideal book to be used in small groups or for personal study and devotion.

Simon Robinson is the senior minister of Walton Evangelical Church, Chesterfield, England. He has also written several other books, all published by Day One, including *Jesus, the life-changer, Improving your quiet time, Opening up 1 Timothy,* and *God, the Bible and terrorism.* He also preaches and teaches in Asia and the United States. He and his wife, Hazel, have two sons and one grandson.